How to Develop a Retention Schedule

by
John Montaña

INTERNATIONAL®

ARMA International
Overland Park, Kansas

Consulting Editor: Mary L. Ginn, Ph.D.
Composition: Gray Design
Cover Art: Cole Design and Production

ARMA International
11880 College Blvd., Ste 450
Overland Park, KS 66210
913.341.3808

ISBN: 978-1-931786-76-8
Catalog No. A4912

Contents

Preface

In the records and information management (RIM) business, meeting people with no records management background at all, who have just been appointed the records manager of their organization, is a common occurrence. One of the first things the newly minted records manager is often tasked with is the development of a records retention schedule; and so of course, the questions urgently come to her/his mind: "What's a retention schedule?" "What does it look like?" "How do I go about creating one?"

If you are in that or a similar situation, *How to Develop a Retention Schedule* was written with you in mind. In this book, I'll tell you what a retention schedule is and set forth the process by which to create one, from data collection to drafting and structuring it, to developing retention periods. By the end of the book, you should have a good idea of what you need to do to get that retention schedule drafted, and what you need to keep in mind to make sure it is up to snuff. Sample forms that will help you get started are included in the appendices.

In the body of the book, I've avoided—as much as possible—legal jargon, technical terms, citations to authority, and some of the other things that you might expect in a treatise or scholarly work. I think that for the beginner, a better approach is to set forth a clear and straightforward explanation of retention schedules and the process of creating one, leaving the scholarly reading for another occasion. On the other hand, bear in mind that a large body of scholarly and technical writing is available, as well as laws and standards, on the topic of retention scheduling. That being the case, I've included lists of additional reading in the appendices for those readers who wish to explore the topic further.

As an entry-level book, *How to Develop a Retention Schedule* is not intended as the only word on records retention schedules, or even the last word. The process I describe isn't the only way to construct a retention schedule, either. Other practitioners do the same things differently, and the good ones do them well with effective results. Although our approaches all have many things in common, there are differences, and you may find some of the different things in these other approaches valuable. By all means, compare approaches and experiment if doing so seems worthwhile. You may find something of real value to you in one of the other approaches, and you may come up with an innovation of your own that the rest of us haven't thought of.

In the meantime, welcome to the RIM profession. Developing a records retention schedule is only the first of many challenging tasks that will confront you during your time in this field. The field is rapidly growing in both importance and complexity, and as a result, in the sophistication of thought and technique that practitioners apply to resolving the issues that face them. You will find that your time in RIM offers many opportunities to be part of that growth.

Acknowledgments

It takes a village to raise a child, and likewise, it takes a village to write a book. This one is the result of a long process of learning from and with many people: colleagues with whom I have debated and hashed out professional issues, clients with whom I have puzzled through thorny problems, seminar attendees who have posed difficult questions. Each time this situation occurs, we wind up knowing a little bit more, and making whatever it is we are thinking about a little bit better; and all that knowledge went into this book one way or another.

Some folks require individual acknowledgment: Preston Shimer, Paula Harris, Marti Fischer, and Sandie Bradley, who reviewed the manuscript and offered many valuable suggestions that have materially improved it; Vicki Wiler and the skilled and longsuffering staff at ARMA International, who take the scribblings of authors like me and turn them into a real book; Don Skupksy, who got me into this business in the first place; and my colleagues at Pelligroup—George Cunningham, Brent Gatewood, and John Kain—with whom I have collaborated on the 200 or so retention schedules that form the basis of my thoughts on the topic.

All these people have made this book much better than it would otherwise have been. If any errors or weaknesses remain notwithstanding their contributions and assistance, they are mine alone.

Finally, I'd like to acknowledge my wife, Connie, and my children, Lenny and Christina. They have cheerfully endured my many late nights in the office, and the moaning and groaning that inevitably issues from an author on deadline; and Connie has been a valuable professional sounding board throughout the process.

To all of you, my thanks.

Retention Schedule

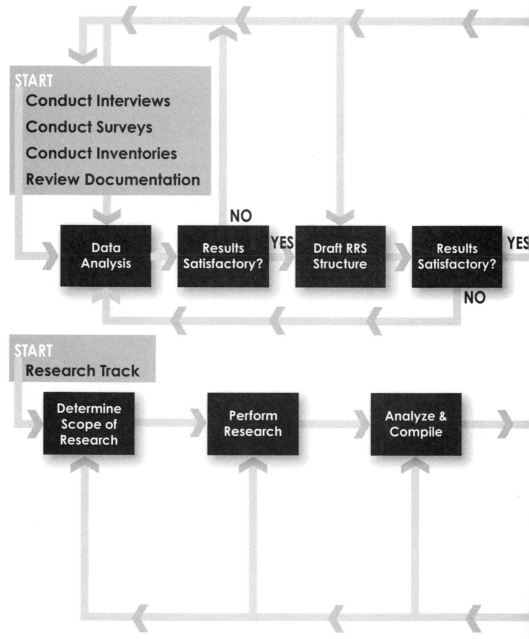

RSS = Records Retention Schedule

Development Flow Chart

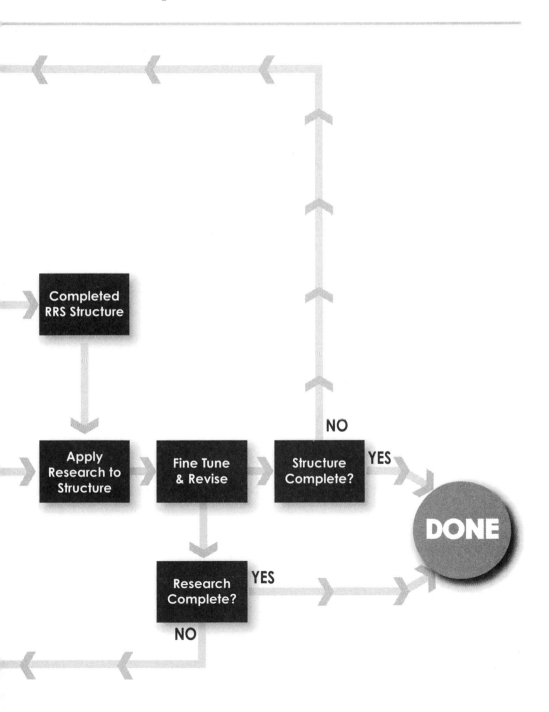

Chapter 1

What Is a Records Retention Schedule? Why Do I Need One?

If you are new to the records management business, you may not be very familiar with *records retention schedules*, what they consist of, or what they are used for. So, before we begin discussing the details of retention schedules, let's spend a bit of time thinking about what they are and why we might need one.

The Fundamental Concept

All organizations have records. In modern society, even the simplest organization cannot function without them. If the organization lasts long enough, it has too many records. The file cabinets are full, the computer files have overflowed onto disks and tapes, and the basement is full of boxes. At this point, the organization must, as a matter of necessity, get rid of some records.

Destroying records is not as easy as simply tossing them out when you run out of space. The most obvious reason is that someone in the organization might still need some of the records you were tempted to toss. Before you do anything about the records, you must therefore at least make some sort of mental calculation that goes something like, "Well, we could still get audited for 2005, so we'd better not throw anything away that's newer than that, or we'll get hit with a penalty."

You just created a records retention schedule. Not a very good or comprehensive one, but a records retention schedule, nonetheless. Additionally, you considered three key factors that all retention schedules must account for:

1. We can't destroy records newer than some date, because we may still need them;

2. Some sort of law may affect this date; and

3. We may have some sort of legal trouble if we don't account for that law.

The retention schedule you created in your mind also contains the fundamental pieces of all retention schedules: a list of records, a retention period for them, and a rationale for that retention period.

What Is in a Records Retention Schedule?

> . . . the schedule has a single, straightforward purpose: it is a document that lists what records are in the organization and how long the organization intends to keep each type of record.

Retention schedules are usually paper or electronic documents rather than mental impressions, and the schedule is usually quite a bit more complicated than our hypothetical schedule. One reason is that your organization probably has more than one kind of record. In addition to accounting records, even a small and simple organization probably has a few personnel-related records. Therefore, the organization has at least two kinds of records and at least two potential *retention periods* to go along them. Scale that up to a very large and complex organization, and it means thousands of record types with potentially thousands of retention periods. The number and kind of rationales for those retention periods increases with size and complexity as well.

Organizations keep records to meet many needs, so beyond the hypothetical tax audit, you might have to consider customer service issues, the possibility of lawsuits, and the need to track financial performance, just to name a few.

With few exceptions, organizations of all types are subject to laws that affect the records they create, how long they keep them, and what they can do with them. For a small and simple organization, those laws may consist of a handful of tax and personnel requirements that affect some simple accounting records and personnel files. Increase the size and complexity of the organization, and both the kinds of records and the number of laws that regulate them increase. At the other end of the spectrum, a very large organization producing complicated products, such as drugs or airplanes, may have many thousands of record types governed by many thousands of laws, and it is affected by very complex business needs and risk management considerations.

A records retention schedule is developed in an attempt to accommodate all an organization's needs and possibly other things as well. However, the schedule has a single, straightforward purpose: it is a document that lists what records are in the organization and how long the organization intends to keep each type of record. At least implicitly, some justification is developed for each retention period chosen.

A good retention schedule may contain a good deal more information than merely records and their retention periods. Rather than being a mere listing, a records retention schedule may:

- Be quite elaborately structured and formatted;
- Have record types that are organized into groups or a hierarchy;
- List additional information about record types such as location or media; and
- Have citations to legal or other authority attached to demonstrate the rationale for retention periods.

In the final analysis, however, a retention schedule is a list of records followed by their retention periods.

The Retention Schedule as Institutional Memory and Marching Orders

If a records retention schedule is just a list of records and retention periods, the question naturally arises, why bother with all the rest? Why not just have the list and the retention periods? Indeed, why bother with a written retention schedule at all? Organizations have several good reasons for preparing a written retention schedule and spending the time to make it a good schedule, with formatting, structure, hierarchy, and documented rationale.

The most obvious of these reasons is that if you don't write down your ideas, bits of your original thinking will be lost over time—you will forget some part of it, or forget why you made some choice, and things won't be done completely, or they will be done incorrectly. Even if *you* don't forget, you won't be around forever, and your replacement would likely find something written down that could be very helpful.

Don't discount the memory factor as a reason for having a written schedule, written filing systems procedures, and other written tools. Discovering that the filing system and the records retention process reside entirely in the brain of a single employee is not uncommon when the records operation of a business, or department of a business, is analyzed. The rest of the business or department is totally dependent upon that one employee to manage records, and if that employee someday becomes an ex-employee, the loss can be a serious problem. Sometimes those ex-employees wind up with a very secure retirement income. They are rehired, because their successors could not figure out what they were doing all those years

> Don't discount the memory factor as a reason for having a written schedule, written filing systems procedures, and other written tools.

and are *still* dependent upon them. Your organization should not and need not be in this situation.

In the meantime, you are not the only one that needs the retention schedule. Other people will probably want to use the same information, and having a written retention schedule makes it easily available to them. That written schedule is a big help to any organization that is faced with the need to dispose of some records. The bigger the organization, the more help the schedule will be—you can easily advise the guy down the hall in person, but advising the business unit in Europe in the same way is less easy.

In this role, a retention schedule is a set of work instructions for the people in your organization: "Keep this record six years, keep that record ten years." In the absence of these written instructions, people may not keep this record for six years and that one for ten years. They may keep them only two years, much to your chagrin when the tax auditor wants to see them. Or, they may take the other approach and keep them all forever, packed into every nook and cranny of whatever space available, and stored in dozens or hundreds of shared drives on your computer system. As a set of written instructions, the retention schedule helps avoid these kinds of scenarios, as well as the necessity for everyone in the organization to consult with you personally every time they want to dispose of an old record.

Retention Schedules and Managing Cost

The practical value of being able to manage this process successfully can be large. A data- or records-intensive business generates substantial quantities of records in the course of a year, and it must all be stored someplace. Active office space and work areas and active computer systems are usually the first choice, but eventually these spaces fill up, and more space must be acquired. Adding office space is expensive, as is adding computer infrastructure; so, most organizations rapidly start looking for other options. Often the best option means entering into a contract with a commercial records storage service, which means that you get a bill every month for storing your old records. You realize at that moment that storing old records isn't free, and the cost is proportional to the volume of your records. Keeping the volume of records in storage under control reduces that monthly bill, and a retention schedule helps accomplish that cost reduction.

The cost of finding things is also an important question. If you have records, persons outside your organization may want to see them, and many of those people have a right to do so. They include the tax auditors in our hypothetical example, as well as judges, lawyers, and bureaucrats. If your organization is a public or government entity, perhaps the public at large also has a right to see the records.

In order to produce those records, your staff must spend time searching through old records to locate them, which can be disruptive and expensive, sometimes very expensive. If the situation in question is a lawsuit or other legal process, the person doing the searching may not be an employee, but instead a paralegal or lawyer from your outside law firm. If the paralegal's rate is $175 per hour, the search process will be even more expensive. If the person doing the searching is not the paralegal but the lawyer, the cost is even more expensive. More records to search through usually means more cost—another strong incentive to keep the volume of material within reasonable bounds. This process of finding records for lawsuits and legal proceedings is called *discovery*, and it is referred to from time to time in this book. Once again, the systematic process of which a records retention schedule is a part can reduce this cost considerably.

The Value of a Formal Document and Program in Dealing with External Parties

Many of these outside parties who seek your records may be interested not only in the contents of your records, but also in what you did with your records and why you did it. In most cases, strong incentives apply to either being able to give them records when they want them, or to being able to prove that you don't have them and aren't required to have them. Those incentives range from a good relationship with the party in question to fines and penalties if you don't have records that you are supposed to have, to some very onerous penalties in lawsuits if a judge decides that you should have important records that you don't have.

A well-drafted and well-documented retention schedule assists you in dealing with all these people. It answers, or perhaps even deflects, questions from them about what records you have and why you have disposed of others, by demonstrating that you have maintained the records you are required to keep for the correct period of time and that you have a legitimate reason for having disposed of them at the end of that time.

A Retention Schedule as a Policy and Compliance Document

A records retention schedule fulfills the following functions:

- **A policy document.** It is your statement of how long you intend to keep particular records, and perhaps some justification for the retention decisions you have made.

- **A set of work instructions.** As noted previously, employees can find out how long they should retain records and when to destroy them.

- **A compliance document.** It demonstrates to outside parties that you are complying with any legal duties to keep particular records for particular lengths of time.

Retention Schedules in Court

Given these functions, the fact that records retention schedules sometimes wind up in court is not surprising. This situation generally occurs because a litigant wants to obtain records from another litigant, and the second litigant does not have them. Whether they *should* have them becomes an issue in the lawsuit, and the records retention schedule is introduced as evidence for the reasoning behind the records' absence. The theory in this case is that having maintained and then destroyed the records in accordance with the policy and directions contained in the retention schedule, the party is therefore excused from having the records. Occasionally, the situation is the other way around: the opposing party attempts to prove that the records retention schedule is merely a smoke-screen used to conceal improper destruction of evidence, and they bring the retention schedule into court with the intent of poking holes in it and demonstrating that it is deficient or worse. Improper destruction of evidence is called *spoliation*, and it is also a concept referred to from time to time in this book.

During the history of records retention litigation, both sides to this argument have had their moments. Taking time to consider what value a records retention schedule has in litigation is worth the effort. Obviously, a records retention schedule has value if constructing and using it properly provides some assurance that you can destroy old records without getting into trouble. On the other hand, that value is considerably diminished if there is much likelihood that the retention schedule will be turned against you, and serious allegations of spoliation or other impropriety result in fines, lost lawsuits, and other bad outcomes.

> Taking time to consider what value a records retention schedule has in litigation is worth the effort.

The Fallacy of Permanent Retention

Given the possibility of a spoliation claim, why don't organizations just keep all old records forever? It might be expensive, but it would avoid or solve many problems—no chance of breaking the law (well, maybe, unless there is a *maximum* retention period in the law someplace) and no allegation of spoliation. What could be simpler? Organizations sometimes try to take this approach, either intentionally or by simply not dealing with the issue. Once in a while, a lawyer suggests that an organization should have kept all its records.

You probably cannot keep old records indefinitely. Sooner or later, you will run out of space, whether physical or virtual, and something has to go. Or, so much has accumulated that when you have to find something for a lawsuit or audit, locating it becomes impossibly difficult or expensive. Or, your employees are so overrun with old records that doing their jobs efficiently becomes difficult or impossible. In all these cases, the pain of not developing and implementing the schedule eventually becomes greater than the pain of doing so; but in the meantime, the size and complexity of the cleanup have become considerably larger. So, unless you have a great deal of space and a great deal of money, you can delay the day when something must be done; but you probably cannot avoid it. In the meantime, people will have taken things into their own hands out of necessity, and little bits of the material you thought would be preserved forever are quietly being destroyed to make room to work. As a practical matter, you need a retention schedule; but you need it to be capable of answering questions about your motives or actions and of withstanding any challenges to its legitimacy.

> As a practical matter, you need a retention schedule; but you need it to be capable of answering questions about your motives or actions and of withstanding any challenges to its legitimacy.

What a Records Retention Schedule Really Accomplishes

In the final analysis, a records retention schedule provides certainty and boundaries to the volume and timeframe of records that are being retained. You know with some certainty what you have and what you don't have, and why. It provides boundaries and certainty to the records that are available, not only for litigation, but also for audits, historical research, and all other purposes. Inside the boundaries, the records are there; outside the boundaries, they are gone. Not to deprive litigants of records, not to hide anything, not to deprive posterity of anything; but because some boundary had to be drawn—and one *was* drawn—and some records fell outside that boundary. If the boundary is prudently chosen, it will withstand any challenge to its legitimacy.

In this role, a retention schedule and its operation are a low-level administrative function, no different from cleaning out the old pallets that have accumulated in a warehouse and prevent the moving in of valuable products or supplies needed to run the business. Just as with old records, someone may someday want those old pallets, but an organization cannot accommodate everybody and let the pallets continue to pile up forever in valuable warehouse space at the expense of business operations. Therefore, the organization will keep as many records as they think that they will need and get rid of the rest. The nature of the modern business and legal environment requires organizations to go to some length to prove that the pallets thrown out are not needed by anyone and that the organization isn't required to keep them; but, in the final analysis, all the organization is doing is throwing out old and empty pallets to make room for new ones full of valuable things. The retention schedule helps organizations throw out the proper pallets at the proper time and prove the propriety of doing so to anyone who questions them about it.

Where to Go from Here

Now you know that you need a retention schedule, you know why, and you have some idea of what it should contain. The next step is to figure out how to construct one. Throughout the rest of this book, the process of developing a retention schedule is examined in detail. This process includes how to acquire the right information, how to analyze and assemble it, and how to assemble it into a records retention schedule.

By the end of the book, you will have a good understanding of how to tackle the process of developing a retention schedule and an understanding of the resources you will need to marshal the process in order to successfully complete the project. You will still have a lot of work to do—building a retention schedule can be a complex project that requires a number of steps to get from initiation to completion, sign-off and publication, and may take a substantial period of time to complete. It also requires the commitment of substantial resources of time and expertise, and the cooperation of many people within your organization. But, you *will* know what information you need to collect, how to get it, and how to assemble that information into a retention schedule that accomplishes the necessary goals and at the same time avoids many common problems.

Chapter 2

Strategic Factors in Drafting and Implementing a Retention Schedule

A records retention schedule is a document that can have important consequences should it become relevant to a lawsuit, audit, investigation, or other serious matter. Those consequences can be either favorable or unfavorable; so, taking time to consider the factors that can influence those consequences is worth the effort. Certainly, the details of the schedule itself are important, and most of this book is concerned with those details. However, even before you reach the details, and as you work them out, there are overall considera tions that you should keep in mind. These considerations are discussed throughout this book.

A Retention Schedule Alone Doesn't Guarantee Anything

A records retention schedule is not, and should not be, considered a blanket insurance policy under which records can be destroyed with impunity and without concern for any legal duties that you may have to preserve records. It *can* offer substantial protection if allegations of spoliation are made, provided that you can establish that the schedule was drafted and implemented in a legitimate manner. Factors that can help establish the legitimacy of your schedule are discussed next.

Retention Periods Should Comply with Applicable Laws

If your retention decisions are called into question, your retention periods must comply with applicable laws, and if you can easily prove that they do, it will be extremely helpful. This reality is the genesis of the custom of documenting, often quite extensively, the legal research and other authority that informs and governs the retention decisions on the schedule. *No* formal requirement that you list citations or can otherwise prove that your retention periods are legitimate exists anywhere; nor is there even a requirement that you know what the legal retention requirements are for your records. If you guess at your retention periods and get them all right, they are good retention periods. Knowing with some certainty that you have chosen sound periods is, however, a good idea. Being able to explain how you arrived at the retention periods that you are using, as well as being familiar with other matters associated with the construction and use of the schedule, are also good ideas. If neither you nor anyone in your organization can explain how the schedule was developed, such lack of knowledge may be taken as evidence that the development and use of the schedule was at least sloppy and negligent, and maybe that it's a cover for spoliation. Consequently, you should be prepared to do some homework.

The obvious way to get around the whole issue of the legitimacy of the retention periods is to choose very long retention periods for everything, but that practice is not free either—longer retention periods mean more records—and very long retention periods mean many more records. The downstream costs add up quickly—the records must be stored someplace, whether in a commercial records facility or in a tape vault, which isn't free. The records must be produced for auditors, for litigation, and for other reasons, which can be very costly. These costs are, in fact, among the very reasons you started drafting a retention schedule in the first place; so, developing a schedule that avoids dealing with this issue is not much of a solution. One of your goals will be to have retention periods that are reasonably short, which means that you must have some understanding of the legal requirements that affect your records so that you can pare down retention periods safely. As long as you have that understanding, you might as well include the legal requirements as part of the documentation of your retention schedule.

Records Destruction Should Be Done in the Normal Course of Business

In other words, the *destruction* of records should occur as a routine, and ideally regularized or cyclic, business process in accordance with the retention schedule. The pattern to be avoided is one that has gotten more than one litigant into trouble: a one-time records destruction event that occurs in suspiciously close proximity to some lawsuit or other legal problem involving the records, giving rise to the implication that destruction of evidence was occur-

> The pattern to be avoided is one that has gotten more than one litigant into trouble: a one-time records destruction event that occurs in suspiciously close proximity to some lawsuit or other legal problem involving the records, giving rise to the implication that destruction of evidence was occurring.

ring. Routine, scheduled destruction of records helps prevent this problem. This concept of routine records destruction clearly implies a regularized normal-course-of-business implementation process after development and publication of the schedule. Merely publishing it and thereafter letting people do as they will without direction or control risks negating whatever advantages are derived from having the retention schedule in the first place.

A corollary of routine, scheduled records destruction is the concept of documenting that regularized destruction. One of the points of having the retention schedule is demonstrating that you're making correct choices. Documenting the actions taken to implement those choices would enable you to say, "We elected to maintain our accounting records eight years, and on such-and-such a date, we destroyed all our accounting records that were older than eight years, and here is our proof." Once again, there's no general requirement that this documentation be done, but to the extent that such proof exists, it bolsters the assertion that the records destruction was done regularly and openly, and it provides some detail on what occurred.

The Retention Schedule Should Not Be Developed to Improperly Destroy Evidence

On its face, this statement might seem painfully obvious, but the point is worth some thought. How can you prove that you didn't have an improper motive in mind when the whole point of a records retention schedule is to destroy records and thereby make them unavailable?

Proper adherence to the first two points above goes a long way toward establishing the proper motives required by point three. By complying with legal requirements, and probably other requirements or considerations as well, you show that your decisions are objectively reasonable. By making the destruction a routine spring cleaning sort of activity, you show that you aren't simply waiting for a lawsuit to arrive before grabbing the retention schedule and turning on the shredder in order to destroy the evidence in the lawsuit.

Other factors come into play, however. You occasionally hear a statement made that the purpose of a retention schedule is "to prevent opposing parties from obtaining records in a lawsuit" or something similar. Such a statement is liable to be taken as proof of bad motives, as are any other statements or activities that may be construed as showing that you are developing and implementing a retention schedule for the purpose of depriving litigants of records or to destroy evidence. Therefore, when allegations of impropriety occur, other policy documents, training material, and e-mail are commonly requested, and depositions of personnel may be conducted in order to determine whether the records retention program was undertaken for improper reasons. If someone associated with the records retention program has made statements that appear to suggest this intention, they are likely to raise serious questions in the minds of future litigants if they become aware of them. Any such statements are needlessly inflammatory. Destruction of old records is a routine administrative process, and a records retention schedule is a routine document for controlling that process. No need to dramatize this process with histrionic statements.

The statement that the purpose of a records retention schedule is to prevent opposing parties from obtaining records in a lawsuit is untrue, and it isn't much of a justification for a records retention schedule, a records retention program, or the destruction of records. Remember that although a records retention schedule authorizes the destruction of records, it also *requires* their retention for some period of time—often a substantial period of years—prior to that destruction. If some litigant wants some records during that period of retention and is legally entitled to obtain them, the retention schedule offers no excuse for not giving the records to them. To the contrary, it tends to substantially increase the likelihood that the records they are seeking will be available to them by providing a clear set of rules that controls any destruction of records. Therefore, as much as anything, a retention schedule is a tool that assists litigants in obtaining records from an organization.

The depriving-litigants-of-records aspect of a retention schedule is probably vastly less prominent as a motive for destroying old records than is sometimes supposed. Most retention schedules arise because, as in the very first example, the excess of old records—and increasingly, of electronic data—uselessly occupying space and infrastructure and burning increasingly large amounts of money in the process, has reached a critical juncture. Something has to be done; so, the retention schedule is born. Organizations in nonlitigious businesses or jurisdictions commonly have a retention schedule for precisely this reason. If any factor related to litigation is prominent in the records retention process, it's the last one: cost. Searching through that sea of old records and data to respond to a subpoena or discovery demand becomes unreasonably expensive. Something must be done to control that cost. A retention schedule is one of the tools for doing so, along with records management software and many other things. Sample records retention schedules are included in Appendix A.

Records Subject to Known Legal Process Must Be Preserved from Destruction

The concept here is simple, but critical: If you become aware that a lawsuit or other legal process has commenced or is likely to commence, records that are

> Although a records retention schedule authorizes the destruction of records, it also requires their retention for some period of time—often a substantial period of years—prior to that destruction.

relevant to that legal process cannot legitimately be destroyed. They must be identified, segregated, and preserved until either the matter is resolved, or it is established to the satisfaction of all parties that they aren't needed.

As a practical matter, this *legal hold* process requires close coordination with your organization's legal staff or outside counsel and with your opponents in the legal proceeding. It also requires some very robust process for making sure that if a legal proceeding arises, knowledge of it is communicated to anyone in the organization who may have records and information relevant to it and for making sure that they find and preserve those records. The details of this process are beyond the scope of this book. Just remember, if you have a records retention program, you must also have a legal hold process.

> **If you have a records retention program, you must also have a legal hold process.**

Review and Approval

The retention schedule is an important policy document whose adoption and implementation have significant implications for the organization. Therefore, you will want to satisfy yourself that what the schedule demands is agreed upon and that the weight of management approval is behind it. Part of the process of developing the schedule should therefore be to include an approval process that includes important stakeholders. Some candidates for inclusion include legal counsel, tax compliance experts, and human resources, but others are likely, depending on the nature of your organization and the particular activities it undertakes.

The Overall View

Your records retention schedule and the program around it should be crafted to be both legal and ethical, and you will want to construct the schedule and document it in a way that makes clear that it is legal and ethical. You can accomplish everything that a records retention schedule needs to accomplish in a completely legitimate and above-board way. That being the case, there's no reason to do otherwise, and no reason not to do so transparently.

Chapter 3

Data Collection

The drafting of a retention schedule is necessarily based on the assumption that you know something about your records. When you're starting the process, however, this assumption probably isn't true. So, you must somehow gain that information in order to build a sound records retention schedule. How do you get that information? Several sources that can be used are discussed next.

A Pre-Existing Records Listing

If you have or can get a list of records that your organization uses, it can be a starting point in the development of a retention schedule. Where can you get one? Your efforts may not be the first attempt at devising a retention schedule for your organization. A schedule may already be in place, or at least drafted. One of your first tasks is to collect any of this material—retention schedules, records lists, file plans, and so on—to determine whether it is suitable as a basis for further work. Even if no prior organizational retention schedule work has been done, some departments or business units may have developed local schedules, or at least local file plans or records listings for their own use. Some may even have departmental retention schedules.

If you have a retention schedule and are contemplating using it, however, you need to exercise some care—pre-existing listings commonly have some weaknesses, and you need to be aware of them, as follows.

- *In all but the smallest organizations, the listing is almost certainly incomplete.* Developing an absolutely complete records listing in a large organization is a formidable and costly undertaking. It involves sending personnel to catalog the contents of every file drawer, every hard drive, every tape, and every box of records, and then analyzing the results of this massive data collection effort. Because of the large number of work hours—and as a result, cost—needed for this project, it is rarely done. Any listing you are in possession of is unlikely to be a result of such a project. If it is not, maybe a great many records will not be listed. If the listing is the sole basis of your schedule, many records will not be accounted for.

- *A surprisingly large percentage of records on a pre-existing list will be meaningless to you and to others.* Records listings come from many places. Occasionally, they are the result of a systematic effort on the part of a person or team with the knowledge and diligence to produce a thorough and meaningful listing. Frequently, they are not. Generally, they're the compiled and largely unedited results of surveys, or compilations of lists produced locally within departments or business units. Or, you may also be working with a list of records that have been boxed and sent to inactive storage.

  In all these cases, the list is the work of many people. Some individuals will have been competent and diligent; some not. The result will be that many record titles and descriptions, if they are present, will clearly indicate what a record is. In other cases, you can make an informed guess. In still other cases, you may be able to hazard a guess; and finally, a remainder—sometimes as much as 20 or 30 percent of the total—cannot be identified. You don't know what a "Form 926" is, nor does anyone else that you contact seeking information about it. Or, an entry is so general as to be useless such as "computer tapes." In either case, you cannot meaningfully assign a category or a retention period.

- *Unless the list has been carefully edited, it will be duplicative.* Lots of people and lots of departments have many of the same records. If your list is a compilation from different sources, it will have many examples of duplicates—organizational charts, for example. In other cases, the entries will have different wording, but they describe the same records—"board meeting minutes," "corporate board meeting minutes," and so on. Duplication makes the list longer than necessary, with the resulting consequences. It also gives rise to the possibility that near-duplicates or analytical duplicates (records that are called completely different things but are really the same record) will receive different retention periods.

These shortcomings are real, but the records listing may be useful in creating a records retention schedule. A listing is often quite useful in helping to develop a sound structure, or in validating one already developed. However, if you have a records listing and are contemplating its use as the basis of a records retention schedule, you should bear in mind these limitations and make adjustments as needed. Almost certainly, you will have to do additional work beyond relying on the listing as-is.

A Records Inventory

Conducting a *records inventory* is the traditional method of gaining the information necessary to analyze and manage information assets. It's a process whose origins are paper-based, and which therefore operates based upon some paper-based assumptions.

As noted previously, a comprehensive inventory is a costly and time-consuming proposition, involving the close examination of massive volumes of records and data. If the resources are available and if the inventory is well-done, it can yield powerful results. If resources are more limited, a records inventory may still be possible, and sometimes necessary, for key repositories of critical or high-risk records.

> If the resources are available and if the inventory is well-done, it can yield powerful results.

Inventories are conducted by assembling a team of personnel whose task is to systematically go through the entire organization (or whatever subset of it is being inventoried), and record every file folder, box, and other data repository it encounters. For each object, the team records information such as location, department, the media on which the record is made, and indexing information that will allow later analysis of the records and development of a comprehensive file plan. If the survey is comprehensive, every file drawer or other container will be opened and its contents cataloged one file at a time. A sample inventory worksheet is provided in Appendix B to give you an idea of what kind of information you will need to capture.

Conducting a large-scale records inventory has several serious drawbacks.

1. **A records inventory is a very time- and labor-intensive proposition.** A single file cabinet may take hours to catalogue correctly, and multiplying this kind of metric over large volumes of data may swamp even an extravagant staffing budget.

2. **Personnel conducting the inventory must be high-quality, trained, and intelligent, if the results are to be at all useful.** Remember that they are looking at files throughout the organization, deciding what the files contain and what they are used for, and assigning them some sort of indexing values based on that analysis. If they don't get it right, the results will be useless. Be selective in choosing your inventory staff, and make sure that they are trained and well supervised.

3. **The inventory describes the state of the records system at a moment in time.** It is sort of a rolling moment, because the inventory is conducted over time. However, the records system is dynamic. Records will come and go and move around. Consequently, your results will become inaccurate over time. If you have inherited the results of a prior inventory, you will discover its inaccuracies rapidly. If it was done years ago, much of it is now invalid.

4. **A comprehensive inventory of electronic records may not be possible.** In theory, electronic repositories should be opened and inventoried as well. (Remember, electronic and paper records are legally and operationally equivalent for almost all purposes.) However, assumptions and drawbacks of the inventory method become apparent when trying to inventory electronic records. In even a moderately large organization, conducting a thorough manual inventory of every hard drive or server is likely to be completely impossible. You might be able to get around this limitation by using computer-generated lists of files on servers or drives. However, leaving aside the volume issue (it could easily be many millions of individual files), electronic files are often very poorly named and organized by their owners. Without information on the contents and use of the files, such a listing would not be very valuable.

5. **A records inventory is sort of a fire-in-the-belly issue.** It sounds like a great idea, and it can yield really useful results; but the initial enthusiasm must be sustained with a long-term budget, long-term staff commitments, and a long-term effort. If these supports start to falter, as often they do as the inventory process grinds forward, the inventory will come to a halt and remain incomplete. Organizations sometimes commence records inventories as a scrap-time project—to be completed by a person or two as they find time—and quickly discover that completing an inventory this way is impossible.

> If a records inventory is valuable and feasible at all, it is so only for relatively small, high-value, and clearly bounded repositories.

If a records inventory is valuable and feasible at all, it is so only for relatively small, high-value, and clearly bounded repositories.

All these things being the case, carefully considering the pros and cons of a records inventory is wise. You are likely to conclude that if a records inventory is valuable and feasible at all, it is so only for relatively small, high-value, and clearly bounded repositories. If you decide to move forward with an inventory, finding a copy of *Information and Records Management*, 4th ed. by Gerald F. Brown, Mary F. Robek, and David O. Stephens, is worth the time and money. Although it was published in 1994 and is now out of print, much of the content is not time-sensitive, including the detailed process of conducting a paper-based records inventory. In any event, be prepared to commit substantial high-quality resources over an extended period of time. If you cannot or won't make this effort, your inventory will not be completed.

> The survey / questionnaire technique offers considerable advantages over a records inventory in terms of the resources needed to conduct it.

Surveys

If you don't have the resources to conduct a records inventory, you may be able to conduct surveys or send out questionnaires. The survey / questionnaire technique offers considerable advantages over a records inventory in terms of the resources needed to conduct it. Rather than teams of personnel fanning out over the organization, only one or two people may be needed to draft the survey / questionnaire, collect them when completed, and analyze the results. This method requires far less staff time, few or no travel costs, and is less susceptible to budget cuts, shifting priorities, and the other pitfalls that await any costly and resource-intensive project.

Conceptually, a survey can be a simple matter and an appealing proposition: you draft the questionnaire, send it out, and await results. As they come in, you aggregate and analyze them, and eventually you have a sound understanding of the organization's records. If you have designed the form correctly and chosen your survey population well, you should have high-quality results. If your organization has an intranet or you have access to survey software, either can be used to make the process even more efficient and painless. Much of the data aggregation and low-level analysis can be automated, leaving you with far more time for the more sophisticated and complex parts of the job. However, a number of shortcomings and obstacles must be overcome, as discussed next.

1. **Identifying the correct personnel to survey can be difficult.** If your organization is large, you will have hundreds or thousands of potential respondents from which to choose. As a practical matter, you probably can't survey them all (and probably don't want to); so, you have to decide which ones need to be surveyed. Making this decision can be a surprisingly difficult task. Identifying the personnel within a department or business unit who know and understand its records thoroughly isn't necessarily something that can be done from looking at an organizational chart. Executives listed on the chart often know little or nothing about records and information management processes, and they may not know who does. Often, the better method is to ask around within a department and get a consensus from departmental personnel about who the local records expert is.

2. **The response rate is often low.** Regardless of what you may think, many of your intended respondents will view their participation as a scrap-time activity. This attitude means that they won't respond at all, or if they do, it will take some nagging. Unless you have considerable pull within your organization, a good many individuals will never respond. If this situation happens in key areas, your data will have important gaps in it. Therefore, you must either have some enforcement mechanism in place to ensure a response, or you must survey additional personnel to provide some redundancy and a cushion, or both.

3. **The response quality can be poor.** When respondents take your survey, one of their chief goals will be to complete it as rapidly as possible so that they can go back to their regular work. Sometimes this objective won't

interfere with providing quality information, but sometimes it will. You will therefore find that some percentage of your responses will be less than fully informative, and some will be more or less useless. You can mitigate this outcome to some extent with a carefully designed survey, but it will always be a problem. Your survey must therefore either be large enough to provide a cushion, or provide for some iterative feedback loop to permit you to follow up and clarify responses when needed.

4.   **The survey form size and the number of questions on it must be limited.** Successful survey procedures include consideration of a practical limit to the amount of time anyone is willing to spend completing a survey. Exceeding that limit will result in fewer responses, lower-quality responses, or both. Consequently, you must limit the time and effort you expect respondents to commit to your survey. The amount of data that you can collect is likewise limited. Problems that arise from the limited amount of data collected can to some extent be mitigated by carefully choosing the data points included in the survey form, but any survey will necessarily be limited in scope and in the quality and depth of the resulting data.

5.   **Developing a high-quality survey form can be challenging.** Any survey will necessarily include a standard set of questions given to all respondents. At best, it might have two or three variations for different sets of respondents. Therefore, your survey will, in many cases, be unable to capture information and issues unique to individual departments or areas of business. This lack of important information in turn may prevent you from optimizing the part of the retention schedule applicable to those departments. An overall survey quality issue is that the quality and detail of responses will be driven by the quality and detail of the questions asked. Questions must be carefully drafted to extract information of maximum value and detail within the limits of the space available on the survey form and the amount of time personnel can reasonably be expected to spend completing the survey. Insofar as possible, questions should be drafted to avoid giving respondents the opportunity to give vague or useless responses and to extract the particular data points needed to construct the records retention schedule. A sample survey worksheet is provided in Appendix C to give you an idea about the kinds of questions to ask.

The results of the interview can be considerably more informative and detailed than can be obtained from a standard survey form.

Interviews

Another common data collection tool is the interview. As compared with a survey, interviews offer some advantages. Once interviewees are in the room (or on the phone), they can't avoid answering the questions; and the personal presence of the interviewer permits immediate follow-up when an answer is nonresponsive, requires clarification, or suggests additional questions. Perhaps most importantly, each interview can be tailored to the particular person and the records involved. The results of the interview can be considerably more informative and detailed than can be obtained from a standard survey form. Of course, the following issues must also be considered:

- *Time.* A records retention project in a large organization could easily involve 50 to 100 interviews or more. Each interview will take an hour or two, not including any travel time, time spent organizing interviews, aggregating and analyzing interview results, and all the other activities surrounding the interviews. These activities can rapidly add up to hundreds of work hours, and if the organization has several locations, a substantial amount of travel.

- *Scheduling.* Individuals that you want to interview have other activities taking up their time; and the higher up they are, the busier their schedules will be, and the harder to corner them for an interview. Rather than lining up in a nice, convenient, consecutive block of time over a period of a couple of weeks, interviews will often be spread over a number of weeks or months, and the investment of travel time and aggravation will be increased. If motivation flags, resources may be redirected, or it was a scrap-time project to begin with, and your interviews may never get completed.

- *Identification of correct interviewees.* As with a survey, interview results will be dependent upon identification of and participation by personnel who are knowledgeable about records and records issues. As a general proposition, you want to interview personnel from every important operational area or business unit, with emphasis on high-risk or high-value areas. Beyond that, however, you want personnel with real knowledge of records and records processes, and identifying these people can be a challenge.

As with surveys, org charts or telephone directories probably won't yield the correct personnel in all cases, requiring some detective work on the part of the interview team. If a survey form is returned with useless information, another form can always be sent to someone else, with little overhead. Flying across the country for a day of interviews only to discover that the interviewees that have been lined up can't really provide the information you need, or even more annoyingly, don't show up for the interview is far more frustrating and a far greater waste of time and resources.

- *Employee resistance to participation.* Employees are sometimes reluctant to participate in interviews. High-level personnel in particular often try to avoid participation by sending administrative assistants in their place. That practice may be fine if the replacement personnel are knowledgeable, but often they are not. Therefore, some mechanism must be in place to ensure that the personnel who are identified as the target personnel actually participate in the interview. Additionally, a mechanism must be in place to reassure those who are reluctant to provide information that will otherwise ensure their cooperation.

- *Interviewer quality.* As with a survey, an interview's results are only as good as the questions asked. Interviewers must be trained, intelligent personnel who are knowledgeable about both records and the records retention issues that are likely to arise within your organization. They must also be good interviewers who are insightful enough to recognize when follow-up is required or when an answer suggests an entirely new line of questions. Personnel with these qualities are always in short supply. You may either have to train them or hire specialists for the project. A sample interview worksheet is in Appendix D.

Choosing a Data Collection Method

Which, or more likely which combination, of the methods discussed that you choose will be determined by the resources and time available to you. Few resources and the need for a quick turnaround may limit you to surveys and perhaps some analysis of pre-existing records lists. A bit more resources and time may allow you to supplement the survey with a few key interviews. Still more time and some skilled staff may permit you to skip the survey and conduct really comprehensive interviews. If you are in a high-risk / high-value environment and have some real budget, you may be able to conduct inventories in key areas.

The key to deciding is being realistic about the time, money, skill, and other resources that you have available, while recognizing that if you go cheap-and-cheerful, your results won't be as good or as comprehensive as they might otherwise have been. However, if you overestimate your available resources, your project will stall. Therefore, take a good hard look at your resources, and decide what's really possible. Then, the decision becomes a balancing act—each technique is potentially useful. Your goal is to use the resources in a combination that maximizes the return on your investment of resources.

What Information Is Needed?

Well, information about records, obviously. But exactly what? To some extent, that depends on your overall goals, but some things will be absolutely necessary.

1. **You need as complete a list of the kinds of records that your organization generates, receives, and uses as you can get.** This list will in some cases consist of lists of specific records—Form 1, Form 2, and so on—but in other cases, particularly if you use surveys or interviews, it will consist

of more general information—air pollution monitoring data, or quality control records. In either case, you will need enough information and enough detail to construct *records series*, which are groups of related records that are evaluated as a unit for retention purposes.

2. **Simply getting a list of records or of kinds of records won't permit you to construct a useful retention schedule.** Many of the records may not mean much to you unless you are very familiar with the organization's records and processes, which means that you won't be in a position to assign them meaningful retention periods. Getting a survey response that tells you that some department has MSHA Form 7000-1s may therefore be of little value. You also need to know several other things about an MSHA Form 7000-1. During this process is when you will begin to find out whether your data gathering efforts were adequate, the questions you asked probing enough, and your own knowledge of records management is up to the task. If it isn't, you may have some homework to do.

What Kind of Information Is Recorded on the Record? What Is It Used for?

The categorization of a record and ultimately its retention period are driven by the kinds of information it contains and how it is used. Therefore, your information gathering must not only capture the name of the record, but also capture some useful description of the kind of information that it records. That information need not necessarily be greatly detailed, but it should give you a sound understanding of what is being recorded on a record.

You must also understand why the information is being recorded. What is the purpose of the record? Who looks at it down the road? Why do they look at it? What business process does it support? Answers to these questions provide key bits of information, and if your data gathering doesn't capture them, you will have difficulty developing a sound schedule. Let's consider why this information is so important.

A MSHA Form 7000-1 is used to record accidents, injuries, and illnesses of personnel working in mines. This information is captured because it is required by law. If a mine inspector visits the mine and these records are not available for inspection, the organization can be fined. Otherwise, the purpose of the information collection on a MSHA Form 7000-1 is to assist in identifying hazards and patterns of injuries in mines, and thereby to assist mining regulators and mine operators in developing safe mining practices. If an incident occurs at a mine, these forms may become involved in lawsuits, investigations, and other legal matters surrounding the incident.

Quite a lot of information about a MSHA Form 7000-1 was captured in the previous short paragraph, and all that information is important. Remember that for each records series on your retention schedule, you will need to establish some period of time for retention of the record; and to do that, you need to identify the key factors that identify the nature of the record and its use. Five things of interest about a MSHA Form 7000-1 identified in the previous paragraph include:

1. It involves mines and mining;
2. It records workplace illnesses and injuries;
3. It is a record required by law;
4. It is used to assist in safety analysis; and
5. It may be needed in lawsuits or investigations.

Consider the first point. If you conduct a survey and some location reports back that it has MSHA Form 7000-1s on file, you now know that they are running a mine. If your organization is large and complex, you may not have known that it owned a mine, just like you didn't know about the Class III railroad running at one of your large factories, or about an off-shore captive insurance company in Bermuda, both of which require the capture of specialized data on specialized records unique to their activities for the retention schedule. Once you know that a mine or a railroad or an insurance company is out there somewhere, a whole new area of inquiry opens up—mines, railroads, and insurance companies are heavily regulated, records-intensive places.

Of course, other ways of finding out these things are available, and you may have discovered them through other means. However, your knowledge of what records do is a key tool in your ability to both understand your organization and develop a retention schedule for it. If at the end of the day, you don't understand the significance of what having a MSHA Form 7000-1 means, your retention schedule will have a very large gap in it.

> Your knowledge of what records do is a key tool in your ability to both understand your organization and develop a retention schedule for it.

The other points are equally instructive. If a record is required by law, it probably has a legal retention period that you will need to research and identify. The fact that a form is used to record injuries and illnesses and that it is useful in safety analysis, investigations, and lawsuits should lead to some analysis of the need to retain and manage the record with these considerations in mind. Collectively, these factors help identify a suitable retention period for the record.

How Long Is the Record Needed?

Any record is retained for several reasons. None of those reasons is necessarily the driver of retention. Even if a record has a clear legal retention period, other factors may demand that it be retained longer. A large percentage of the records in most organizations will not have a clear, explicit, legally required retention period. You must therefore have a good understanding of the other reasons that a record may be kept for some period of time. A nonexhaustive list might include the following:

- Day-to-day business operations;
- Tax requirements;
- Customer service;
- Employee service;
- Budgeting and forecasting;
- Strategic planning;
- Regulatory inquiries;
- C.Y.A. (you know what I mean);
- Lawsuits and investigations; and
- Questions from important people within the organization.

One goal of your data gathering must be to identify which of these reasons (may be more than one) is applicable to every record type turned up in the course of the data gathering, and for how long each such consideration applies. So, if you learn that your organization routinely signs tax audit extensions and has open tax years going back ten years, or that the strategic planning window is five years, you're able to get some sense of how long records related to these processes have value to the organization.

However, just collecting the numbers as opined by personnel will not be enough. Remember, the longer you keep a record, the more it costs you in several ways. Therefore, any soft retention consideration (that is, other than a legally required retention period) must be weighed against the cost of accommodating that consideration. You must get some sense of how valuable each such consideration is to the organization for each kind of record. Simply asking how long a record is kept, or how long it is needed, won't provide the information you need. The reason is that many people entertain one or more of several fallacies about their records that tend to result in answers with retention periods much longer than are really needed. For example:

- They overestimate the real, ongoing value of their records;
- They assume that legal retention periods are much longer than they actually are;
- They assume that they must be able to answer any inquiry, regardless of how unreasonable or how old the information requested;

- They assume that the legal risks surrounding their records extend much further into the past than they really do;

- They are simply afraid to dispose of old records; or

- Their assumptions about risk are based upon purely hypothetical worst-case scenarios, or some past one-in-a-million occurrence.

Consequently, rather than simply asking, "How long do you need this record?," you must instead pose a series of questions designed to tease out the real value of the record to the organization and its business processes. If it is involved in any risk-based scenarios, such as litigation, you need to know the real extent, time, and value of those scenarios. Once you have this understanding, you are in a position to weigh the extent to which any soft consideration should be accommodated with a longer retention period than is absolutely necessary.

The result of this entire process is straightforward. You should know what records are in your organization and have a good idea of what they are used for, how long they are needed, and why.

Other Information

As long as you are taking the trouble to collect all this information and build a retention schedule, you may decide to collect additional information and perhaps permit your retention schedule to do double duty. You don't need to, of course—a records retention schedule is a list of records along with retention periods for them—and most other things are optional. But if you decide to collect additional information, the questions then become what information do you collect and what do you do with it.

Any number of things about your records could potentially be collected and listed on a records retention schedule. A short list might include the following:

1. Media information—whether the records are electronic, paper, or microform;

2. Locations for records repositories, or the systems on which electronic records reside;

3. The system or software used to manage an electronic records repository;

4. Office of record or official copyholder—the department or business unit responsible for maintaining the record for the official retention period; and

5. *Office retention* versus *total retention*—how long records are to be kept in active office areas.

One thing that may prove really valuable down the road if you keep it up-to-date is the listing of systems and locations for electronic records repositories. In the United States, the Federal Rules of Civil Procedure require that you provide an opponent in a lawsuit this information early in the suit, and having it collected and organized in advance saves time and effort during the lawsuit—particularly valuable if your organization is routinely involved in litigation.

Whether anything else is useful enough to justify the effort involved is something you will have to determine based upon your own needs. Remember, regardless of how you collect your information, this electronic records information is more data that must be collected, potentially meaning a longer survey, longer interviews, or some additional data collection effort. Given that practical time and resource limitations apply in each case, the collection of this information competes against the collection of other information, and something may have to give.

Remember also that once the information is collected, aggregated, and analyzed, it is competing for real estate on the screen or paper, and at some point you'll have to choose among competing data unless you are willing to live with a retention schedule in an awkward format or awkward paper size, or lots of scrolling back and forth on a screen, or hiding and unhiding columns.

If you decide you want to consider adding some of these additional data points, give careful consideration to the real value of any such items. For example, some records series are commonly designated as *vital records*—records whose existence is critical to continued functioning of the organization, and which should therefore be given special treatment and protection. However, unless your schedule has very small, very tightly bounded records series, only select individual records or subunits within the series are vital, not the entire series. Designating an entire series, particularly a broad one, as "vital" may be serious (and seriously costly) overkill.

Likewise, designating a records series as "Sarbanes-Oxley records" sounds attractive, but it may be less meaningful than you suppose. Unless you are one of your organization's financial auditors or you have spent considerable time talking to one, you probably can't make this determination with any accuracy. If you can, it's probably unnecessary anyway—people who need records for Sarbanes-Oxley compliance probably don't need you telling them what they need, and the retention period you select should accommodate Sarbanes-Oxley needs regardless of any designation. As with vital records, the items of interest are liable to be subunits of your series rather than the series as a whole. Of course, if you are designating items as Sarbanes-Oxley Act records, what about the Taft-Hartley Act, the Securities and Exchange Act of 1934, the Canada Income Tax Act, the French Civil Code, or the many other laws—hundreds or thousands of them—that are equally important to your organization? Shouldn't you list them also? If you do, what additional value do they bring?

> Unless your schedule has very small, very tightly bounded records series, only select individual records or subunits within the series are vital, not the entire series.

Your first goal is
to provide clear
guidance for peo-
ple on how long
they should keep
their records—
everything else is
secondary.

Your first goal is to provide clear guidance for people on how long they should keep their records—everything else is secondary.

The answer may be that they don't bring much value at all. Therefore, before you decide to capture a lot of additional nonretention information and clutter your schedule with lots of data points and designations and codes for this and that, think very hard about the actual utility they will provide someone in the future. Remember, your first goal is to provide clear guidance for people on how long they should keep their records—everything else is secondary. Anything that materially interferes with or confuses this information should be left off. Anything else should be added only if it provides real, useful, targeted guidance to someone, on a substantive issue. If it doesn't do this, it is just clutter.

Chapter 4

An Overview of Structuring a Records Retention Schedule

Organizational Complexity

As noted in Chapter 1, a records retention schedule at its simplest is a list of records followed by some indication of how long they should be kept. Also noted, in a very small, simple business, staff might be able to guess at the kinds of records they have in order to make up the list. In this case, the retention schedule might look something like this:

Ace Pizzeria Records Retention Schedule	
Accounting	10 years
Personnel Files	5 years
Delivery Records	2 years

If Ace Pizzeria is a small business with a few employees, a schedule of this sort might be perfectly adequate, assuming that the retention periods chosen were adequate. Assume, however, that the business in question is not Ace Pizzeria, but Acme Foods, a manufacturer of frozen pizzas, and that it employs 20,000 people in thirty states and in a couple of Canadian provinces.

A large company like Acme Foods will have a much more complicated set of business records than will the pizzeria. For example, all the pizzeria's accounting records will likely reside in either a handwritten ledger or on a small business accounting software package. In contrast, Acme Foods will have something like the following:

- A general ledger system, probably electronic;

- An accounts payable system that is partially paper (incoming invoices and some internal paperwork) and partially electronic (captured data about the invoices that feeds the general ledger system);

- An accounts receivable system that is partially paper (returned invoice stubs, incoming checks, and so on), and partially electronic (the invoice generation system);

- An inventory system that may be electronic, paper, or both;

- An order-taking and processing system;

- A payroll system;

- Banking records; and

- A reporting system that pulls data from the other systems and writes accounting reports.

Other records may exist as well. A substantial number of documents that may not be considered formal accounting records are also likely, but they may nonetheless have accounting and tax implications, and so must be included in any determination of accounting and tax records retention periods. A short list of these records might include the following, among others:

- Depreciation schedules for capital property and equipment;

- Credit documents containing information on credit extended to Acme or by Acme to customers or others;

- Contracts of various kinds;

- Spreadsheets and other analytical documents on hard drives or in file cabinets;

- Past tax returns and supporting documentation;

- Pension and benefit records; and

- Customs and border control records (remember, Acme Foods operates in at least two countries).

Undoubtedly, more records may be available, but you no doubt get the idea. What can be styled simply as "accounting records" in a very small situation becomes a very complex set of records in a large and complex operation. This analysis is equally true of human resources. A personnel record at the larger company is likely to be a good deal more complex. However, if Acme Foods offers medical and retirement benefits, has employees who are subjected to some types of workplace hazards, receive formal training, or are subject to other specialized legal requirements, there may be additional complexity as well.

Then there's the rest of the business. Both organizations have something that might be called an "operations department." In the pizzeria, that department consists of a telephone and an order taker, a pizza oven and a pizza maker, and a car and a driver. In a small pizza parlor, the order taker and pizza maker might even be the same person. When it's really slow, all three might be the same person. The workflow is simple—an order is taken, a pizza is made, and it is sent out for delivery. When pizza supplies are needed, the owner picks them up on the way to work in the morning. Everything else is outsourced.

Once again, things are much more complex in a larger organization. The same workflow to deliver a pizza to a customer requires the following, among other things:

- A sales and order-taking system;
- A receiving department for supplies;
- A warehouse for supplies and raw materials;
- A shipping department for sending out finished goods;
- A motor pool to manage and service the truck fleet delivering finished goods;
- A large, complicated food production factory;
- A warehouse for finished goods; and
- A quality assurance lab to test both raw materials and finished goods.

Once again, there will be other things as well. A large industrial operation such as Acme Foods will have engineers, electricians, plumbers, millwrights, food scientists, and others not found in the pizzeria. The organization may also have many other support departments such as marketing and advertising, a law department, an environmental quality department, a computer services department, a security staff, and so on. All these departments will generate records of one sort or another, and these records will be needed for varying lengths of time, depending upon the kinds of records, what uses they have to the business, and what laws, if any, may require their retention.

Considerations in Developing a Structure

Several things affect the structure of a records retention schedule, including:

1. **The complexity of the retention schedule will vary depending on the size and complexity of the organization.** Even though they may accomplish the same basic function, in a larger organization, the records are inherently more complex. The larger organization will also have records not found in the smaller organization because the web of support functions is smaller in a smaller organization. Perhaps most importantly, in a larger organization, records may not be kept in a manner that allows you to plop them into a single bucket labeled "accounting."

2. **The larger the organization, the more complex the web of supporting services and departments needed to support its core operations.** In this example, both organizations make pizzas. In the pizzeria, most or all employees make pizzas. At Acme Foods, most employees don't make pizzas. They work in supporting operations for the pizza production facility.

3. **In order to really understand the records generated by an organization, understanding its operations, including both core and support operations, is necessary.** If all you knew about Acme Foods is that they make pizzas, you might conclude that they have accounting records, personnel files and pizza-making records; and as far as that goes, you would be right. But you would miss the hazardous waste records from the motor pool, the salmonella testing records from the lab, that $50 million contract to sell frozen pizzas to the Air Force, and a lot of other things; and you might not want to miss them.

The Need for a Structure

In order to build a retention schedule, you obviously need some list of records, or at least some idea of what records you might have. The previous chapter discussed how you might go about acquiring the right information. Assume here that your data collection efforts were successful and that you are in possession of some sort of records listing to be used as the basis for a retention schedule. Now that you have it, you can use the list to move forward to develop some sort of hierarchy or structure, much like an index or table of contents. You could, of course, skip the whole business of building a systematic structure and just go with a records listing, but there are some reasons not to:

1. **A reasonably complete records listing will be very long.** In a large organization, the number of individual record types could run into the tens of thousands. Even a not-very-complete list could easily run to over a thousand record types. That's a lot of choices when you're trying to decide whether it's okay to destroy an old file. The more complete and accurate your list, the worse the problem will be.

2. **An as-is listing will be in alphabetic or form number order, or no order at all, which is not very useful.** An alphabetic or form number list of records is based on two assumptions: (1) the record has a formal title and/or number, and (2) the person making the inquiry knows what it is. Even if both assumptions are true, it's not a very efficient use of employees' time to scroll down a list of 2,000 items, and then scan and read through 300 unrelated entries under "V" to find "vouchers." If either assumption isn't true, they have to guess what their record might be, which requires them to read all or most of the 2,000 item list, hunting for

a promising candidate. If they're willing to do this, you will have wasted a great deal of their time. If they are not, the record will not be properly assigned a retention period, with whatever results accrue from that decision. The issue of analytical duplicates (records that contain the same or very similar information and are used for very similar purposes but have different names) and near-duplicates also compounds the time-wasting issue—a record could be under "B" for board meeting minutes, or perhaps under "C" for corporate minutes, and may be in other places as well, requiring users to hunt around in all the likely places. If the list is large, that sort of hunting around can be very time consuming and may effectively discourage people from using the schedule. If you haven't carefully edited your list, this sort of thing won't just be a possibility either—there will be many duplicates, near-duplicates, and analytical duplicates.

3. **Even a complete records listing will change over time.** The reason that no one knows what a Form 926 is may be that the company stopped using it in 1971. This situation is often the case with mystery records, and it shouldn't be surprising. Whatever your organization does, its processes and activities, and the way it collects information to record those activities, change over time as well. As a result, old records are no longer used, and new records are created to fulfill new needs. If you elect to use a records listing as your retention schedule, situations like this become your problem. You have taken on the responsibility of somehow keeping your listing completely up-to- date for as long as your records retentions schedule is used to accommodate this process of change. Unless you are extravagantly endowed with manpower and money, and maybe not even then, you will be unable to fulfill this responsibility.

Dealing with the number and complexity of a larger organization's records becomes a good deal easier if some organizing is done by creating categories for the records so that the accounting records wind up in one place, the personnel records in another, and so on. Likewise, within each of these categories, smaller categories could be created for the various subkinds of each category. If done right and the records are put into these categories, finding a particular record, or guessing where a particular record might sit on the schedule, becomes much easier. That important step makes everyone's life easier. You can now begin to see the value of a well-constructed records structure. Benefits include:

- *A records structure is an insurance policy in case every record is not identified.* Each category and subcategory in the schedule captures within it some group of records, perhaps many records. "Personnel files" for example, may include a large assortment of individual records, including applications and resumés, demographic information, benefits elections, performance reviews, and so on. If a record is overlooked, an obvious category, such as "personnel files," makes it far more likely that an inquirer will make the proper choice.

Each category and subcategory in the schedule captures within it some group of records, perhaps many records.

- *A records structure makes the schedule shorter and easier to search.* A well-developed structure can reduce the number of potential choices for a searcher from thousands to much fewer. Depending upon the philosophical and practical choices made when developing the schedule, the number of categories might run from one hundred to perhaps three or four hundred. Not only will the number of categories be smaller, but also the categories themselves will be laid out in a logical manner—accounting records in one place, human resources records in another. In combination, these categories are powerful tools. Searchers will spend much less time perusing the schedule and will make more accurate choices.

- *The records categories will not change as much over time.* Form 926 may go out of use, but accounts receivable will not. So if Form 926 is an accounts receivable form, and it is replaced by Form 927, a searcher, knowing that Form 927 is about accounts receivable, can easily and correctly categorize the form.

Determining the Structure

One you have decided that a mere list is inadequate, you must then determine the basis for the structure you will build. Commonly used candidates are discussed next.

The Departmental Schedule

In the departmental retention schedule model, the retention schedule is effectively a list of the departments or business units of the organization, with the records managed by each unit listed. A departmental retention schedule for an organization might look something like this:

Records must be listed for each department that maintains them, often a number of times, resulting in a [departmental] schedule that is both duplicative and longer than it would otherwise be.

- Accounting
- Corporate Secretary
- Human Resources
- Manufacturing
- Motor Pool
- Shipping and Receiving

Beneath each top-level term is a list of records, or perhaps subheaders based upon subunits of the department or in some sort of categorization by record type. A departmental schedule has a few noteworthy shortcomings:

- *It will be duplicative.* Many common record types are maintained by multiple departments such as in accounting and human resources departments. These records must be listed for each department that maintains them, often a number of times, resulting in a schedule that is both duplicative and longer than it would otherwise be.

- *It may result in inconsistent retention periods.* Unless care is taken, a record, say an invoice from a benefits service provider, may receive a different retention period in the accounting department than the one it has in human resources. Consequently, after some point, only an incomplete set of invoices is likely to exist. This inconsistency is undesirable, because it causes uncertainty and may hamper activities such as audits. It's also a common basis for complaints that the retention schedule is a cover for improper activity, and thereby raises the specter of a spoliation claim.

The Functional Schedule

In the *functional retention schedule* model, records are grouped into categories based upon the use of the record and the kind of information it contains. Regardless of where the records are located or who maintains them, records containing the same kind of information fall into the same category. Thus, accounts payable invoices are listed only once, and every department that maintains copies of them uses that listing to determine their retention period. The schedule is shorter, and a good deal of duplication is eliminated. These factors, collectively, make for an easier-to-use and more effective schedule.

A functional schedule has another key strong point: laws governing records retention do so on a functional basis. If a tax law governs the retention of invoices, it governs them regardless of the department they may reside in. Separate and different retention periods for invoices are not maintained by different departments. A functional schedule with its single entry for each record type permits the assignment of uniform retention periods and avoids the temptation to assign a different retention period to a department due to office politics or similar reasons, or simple oversight.

A functional schedule does have one commonly seen drawback: on a functional schedule, a single department's records may be spread throughout the schedule based upon their functional use. In and of itself, this is not a bad thing once you're used to it. However, users that are unfamiliar with retention schedules, on first being exposed to one, commonly expect to see all the records maintained by their department in a single place—they expect a departmental schedule. When confronted with a functional schedule, they often take some time to adjust to it before they are comfortable with the functional classification scheme. Planning some familiarization training into the rollout of a functional schedule may be necessary to permit personnel to gain familiarity and comfort with it.

If you compare a functional to a departmental schedule, they may appear to be the same, and indeed, superficially, they often appear similar. On both

> On a functional schedule, a single department's records may be spread throughout the schedule based upon their functional use.

schedules, there will typically be such categories as accounting and human resources. However, in the detail, they can be quite a bit different, even though they contain the same records and record types. This discussion focuses on functional schedules. Readers desiring to simulate a departmental schedule can always easily do so after having developed a functional schedule. The process for doing so is easy: having developed your functional schedule, you simply create excerpts of it for different departments, having excised the parts not relevant to them. Staff in all departments are all still looking at the same schedule, just not the whole thing.

Building the Structure

Once you know something about your records, you can begin building a structure. For example, you may have a list of some accounting records such as:

- Incoming invoices,
- Outgoing invoices,
- Ledger,
- Vouchers,
- Timesheets,
- Check register.

You can create hierarchy for this list by analyzing the use of each record. Once you have determined what each record is used for, you can then build a structure that reflects those different uses. In this example, all the records are accounting records; so, "Accounting" is a logical top-level term. Sublevels are then determined by analysis of what each kind of record is used for. The result might look something like this:

Accounting
    Accounts payable
        Incoming invoices
    Accounts receivable
        Outgoing invoices
    Banking
        Check register
    General Ledger
        Ledger
        Vouchers
    Payroll
        Timesheets

> Once you have determined what each record is used for, you can then build a structure that reflects those different uses.

Additional records can be placed within the categories (the categories are, in records management parlance, "records series"), and when a record comes along that does not fit into any category, a new category or subcategory (or "subseries") can be created to accommodate it. Eventually, as you acquire a complete listing of accounting records, your hierarchy is fully built out with all the needed categories and subcategories.

An alternative way is to start with categories or series. If you know something about accounting, you can make educated guesses about the likely categories of records—payables, receivables, general ledger, and so on—found in an accounting records system. As you obtain information about individual record types, map them into your hierarchy, making adjustments to the hierarchy when it becomes apparent that you have missed something. You should eventually end up in the same place as you would have using the first method.

Note however, that in both cases, the categorization can only be done if you understand the use to which each record and each record type is assigned. Even if you are starting from a pre-existing listing, you will probably have to put a good deal of effort into understanding what function the various records on your list perform during their working life. If you're very familiar with your organization's operations, you may be able to avoid this work for many records, but if not, don't underestimate the amount of time and effort categorization may take.

> Categorization can only be done if you understand the use to which each record and each record type is assigned.

How Much Structure? How Many Levels?

How much structure is enough? Is two levels enough, or should you go with a four-deep index? Should you list every individual record title in its category? As you are building your structure, you'll starting thinking about these and similar questions, and you will have to resolve them prior to finalization of your structure. How you resolve them will affect how useful and user-friendly your schedule will ultimately be.

When considering these issues, an important point to bear in mind is that there is no hard-and-fast rule about how a structure is built, nor is there a single optimal solution that works best in all situations. Every potential option involves some tradeoffs in which you gain some point of functionality at the expense of something else. In working through the issues, your goal will be to make the tradeoffs that minimize the most important downsides and maximize the most important upsides. Assuming, of course, that you know what the upsides and downsides are.

> There is no hard-and-fast rule about how a structure is built, nor is there a single optimal solution that works best in all situations.

For example, consider the number of levels and the number of categories. The tradeoff in this case is simplicity versus accuracy. Consider the following retention schedule:

Records Series	Retention Period
Accounting	15 years
Human Resources	20 years
Operations	50 years

This schedule certainly has the virtue of simplicity. Someone attempting to use it has only three fairly obvious options from which to choose. In most cases they will be able to do so quickly and accurately; so, their time spent consulting it is efficiently and effectively spent. On the other hand, it doesn't provide much information about the kinds of accounting, human resources, and operations records that might exist within the organization; so, it isn't much good as a guide or general index. The retention periods are also rather long. Consider now the example of the same schedule with accounting records developed further into a set of accounting subseries:

Records Series Subseries	Retention Period
Accounting	
Accounts Payable	6 Years
Accounts Receivable	6 Years
Banking	6 Years
General Ledger	15 Years
Payroll	7 Years
Human Resources	
Operations	

You now know a good deal more about the particular kinds of records within accounting. If a similar level of detail were included for human resources and operations, you would also be able to look at the schedule and discern a great deal more about the kinds of records in these areas as well. This level of detail also allows the assignment of meaningful information of other sorts to the records series as well, if this is something that you want to do. You might, for example, want to note that the general ledger system resides in a particular software system administered by a particular department or business unit.

All this detail allows you not only to categorize records for retention purposes, but also to answer questions about particular records. So, if a question arises about hazardous waste manifests, you could consult the "Environmental Compliance" section of the "Operations" category to determine what retention period is assigned to this record, and perhaps determine what department is in charge of these records.

Note also that retention periods for the various subseries in accounting have been reduced in most cases from the 15-year period assigned on the first version of the schedule to all accounting records. We can do this in the second example because not every accounting record need necessarily have a 15-year retention period. However, if the two series are lumped together, you have to give them all the longest retention period that you would have given to any one of them, in this case 15 years. By breaking them into subseries, you can assign shorter retention periods to some, perhaps many of them. Extrapolating this approach to human resources and operations records, you could do much the same thing. By breaking high-level categories into smaller records series, you record more detailed knowledge of your records, and you are able to assign retention periods on a more targeted basis, reducing, often substantially, the amount of time that you are retaining some kinds of records. In all cases, you could take this approach even further, by adding more subseries, or by adding a third or even fourth sublevel to any records series, or by doing all these things.

> Fewer records series means fewer and easier choices and quicker use, but at the expense of less available information and longer retention periods.

Of course, there's a tradeoff: the more series and levels that you create, the more complicated the choices every time someone must classify a record. In the first example, three choices were available; eight, in the second example. If you gave human resources and operations five subseries each, you would force a user to choose from among 18 possible decision points to classify a record. Add more subseries or more levels, and the number of possible classification choices rises very rapidly. And, the choices get harder—the more subseries and sub-subseries you have, the more alike the related ones are. By the time you get to a fourth level, the records in adjacent series are very closely related. The trade-off is conceptually simple: fewer records series means fewer and easier choices and quicker use but at the expense of less available information and longer retention periods.

Determining Complexity

Organizations wind up on every part of this easy-versus-detailed spectrum, depending upon their particular circumstances and their preferences in resolving the tradeoffs involved. A very small business, such as the hypothetical pizza parlor, might be able to get by with a handful of broad categories. On the other hand, a pharmaceutical manufacturer, whose records are very complex and subject to very detailed legal controls, inspections by government agencies, and the ongoing prospect of products liability litigation, is likely to have a very detailed schedule that carefully details long lists of complex manufacturing and test records. Other organizations may wind up somewhere in the middle. Here are a few points to bear in mind about complexity:

- *Limit the number of records series categories to facilitate classification.* A retention schedule with more than a few hundred total categories is likely to be too complex for most users. That means that either they won't use it correctly, or they won't use it at all. If you wind up with a thousand records series, you have probably gone overboard. Your organization's schedule is unlikely to require that level of detail.

- *Limit the number of levels or subseries to improve usability.* Even large organizations often get by nicely with two- and three-deep structures. A fourth level is usually only required for specialized record sets with unique handling or legal requirements. That means that if your entire schedule is a four-deep index, it's probably overkill again, and you can probably prune back a good deal of the complexity with no ill effect. More than four levels for even a part of the schedule will in most cases be both unnecessary and far too complex to justify.

- *Limit the lowest level on the schedule. It should be no smaller than the smallest meaningful records series.* Bear in mind that a retention schedule is a set of instructions used to select records for disposition. As a practical matter, that disposition, usually destruction, will occur on the container level. Someone will select a container—a file folder, box, tape, disk, or whatever—and destroy the entire container and all its contents. It's unrealistic to expect that users will open the container and select individual items from it for destruction, particularly if the number of containers is large. It's just too costly and too time-consuming. That means that the lowest level records series on your schedule should point to the container, and not to part of its contents.

As an illustration, consider a personnel file. It typically contains many different documents, a good number of which have legally required retention periods, almost all of which are shorter than the retention period for the file as a whole. It's possible to construct a retention schedule listing all the various documents and assigning them shorter retention periods, but doing so is based on the assumption that someone will periodically cull through hundreds or thousands of personnel files and pick out these individual documents, say performance reviews that are more than three years old. This assumption is simply unrealistic. Regardless of its theoretical merits, no one will do it. So, you assign a retention period at the container level—the entire personnel file. That's as far down as practical reality will permit you to do it.

Note, however, that here again there is no hard and fast rule. For paper records stored in boxes, the smallest practical container size will be whatever can be identified as being in the boxes, which might be nothing more than "personnel records." At the other end of the spectrum, the same documents residing in a well-managed electronic document management system could be managed for retention purposes at a very granular level if the indexing was sufficiently precise. Even here, though, there are practical limits. Even if your technology is capable of managing the individual retention of ten thousand document types, constructing a retention schedule to do this would be a big job and almost certainly unnecessary. Retention requirements can rarely if ever be applied at this granular a level in a meaningful fashion.

> Assign a retention period at the container level.

- *Ensure that the schedule structure can be extended and is flexible.* Once your retention schedule is deployed, you will rapidly have large numbers of records mapped against it. If your needs or strategy change, you will want to either add detail to your schedule by adding series or subseries, or remove unnecessary detail by rolling up series into a larger series. Being able to do the mapping by extending or contracting the existing structure, rather than by significantly altering what's already there is important. If the existing structure is altered, records mapped against the structure must be re-mapped to the new structure, often with a considerable amount of manual intervention. If the number of records to be re-mapped is large, it can be a very painful process.

> Being able to do the mapping by extending or contracting the existing structure, rather than by significantly altering what's already there is important.

- *Choose a schedule format that provides the best display for users.* Regardless of whether your retention schedule is published electronically or on paper, you have a finite amount of real estate upon which to display it. Too many levels and too much other complexity may mean that it won't fit onto standard paper, or that it won't display on a computer screen without a lot of scrolling back and forth. Anything that interferes with ease of use of the schedule or annoys end users is unhelpful in implementing your program.

The bottom line of this discussion is that in deciding on the complexity of your structure, you must consider the upsides and downsides of the various tradeoffs. You then must consider which of those upsides and downsides you care about most: is simplicity and ease of use paramount to you? If so, can you live with the costs that come from longer retention periods? Do you have records that must be tightly managed for regulatory compliance reasons? And so on.

Your goal is to select a structure that best accommodates your organization's needs while minimizing, insofar as possible, the downsides that will inevitably come with any set of choices. The trick is to try to hit the sweet spot that maximizes the overall value of the schedule. Having hit that sweet spot, or at least come close to it, you'll still be left with some downsides that are a direct result of the choices made. These must simply be lived with.

Now that you have structured your records, you need to consider the other information the schedule might contain, and how you might organize and display it. In addition to records series and retention periods, several other kinds of information commonly included on retention schedules are:

- *Numbering schemes for records series.* People like shorthand, and records series titles are often a bit cumbersome for everyday use; so, it's common, though not universal, to see some sort of numeric or alphanumeric scheme applied to the series on schedules in paper, word processing, and similar formats. They tend to be similar: they frequently start out with some sort of alphabet-based character group for the highest level, with number clusters for the subseries and sub-subseries, something like this:

AC-00-00   Accounting

    AC-10-00   Accounts Payable

        AC-10-10   Invoices

These codes make a convenient shorthand, and they are also valuable for container labeling, use as a filing plan, and similar uses. The following items need to be kept in mind when developing such a scheme.

- *The coding scheme should be intuitive and simple.* It's pretty easy to remember that accounts payable is AC-10-10. It's not so easy to remember if accounts payable is AC245.75/4-E3.

- *The scheme should allow for plenty of open spaces between records series at every level.* Sooner or later, you will start adding additional records series. If you have numbered your series consecutively or too closely, you will eventually wind up in a situation where you need to interleave a records series, but you don't have a number for it. Consequently, you must (a) stop using the numbering; or (b) resort to clunky expedients like having an AC-10B or AC-10.1; or (c) renumber the schedule. If you have mapped records to the schedule using the old numbers, you will have to remap them using the new numbers. Avoid such a situation, particularly if large numbers of records must be remapped manually.

- *An externally imposed numbering scheme may be superfluous and unneeded, or a detriment.* If the retention schedule is to be loaded into records management software or some other electronic database, the software will use internally generated numbering for records series, and external numbering may create conflicts. In these cases, the numbers generated by the system may not be convenient tools for records series shorthand, and you will need to rely on the records series names. It's another good reason to put some thought into the names that you give your series and the structure that you apply to them.

Eventually, whether your retention schedule is in a word processing document, a spreadsheet, or a database, the final product will be something that displays as a tabular document with columns for the various bits of information that you have elected to include for each records series. At or near the left side will be the records series titles, followed by descriptions. Nearby on the right will be space for retention periods. At various points will be columns for whatever other information you decide to include. If you have gotten that far, your schedule is ready for further development.

> In electronic records systems, the official copyholder may not be a business unit, but instead a designated system, database, or repository.

Other Possible Information

You *could* add lots of other things to the retention schedule, and some are worth considering. Here are some possibilities:

- *Official copyholder.* Although other variations of this term are used, the most commonly used is "office of record." All variations, however, convey the same concept: a single department, business unit, or other entity is responsible for maintaining specimen copies of each record in the series for the entire duration of the retention period. That entity is the ***office of record***. Everyone else holding copies of these records are holding duplicates, which are presumably governed by some duplicate records policy that permits their earlier destruction. In electronic records systems, the official copyholder may not be a business unit, but instead a designated system, database, or repository. The important thing here is that everyone understands what the official copyholder means. Generally, a policy will state that duplicate records, or convenience copies of records, can be destroyed at the user's convenience. If the official copyholder is unaware of its status, it may destroy records before the retention schedule authorizes their destruction. If everyone else has also been destroying the same records, you will be without records that you are supposed to have.

- *Other information.* Retention schedules sometimes display a variety of other fields or columns. They include notes fields for text explanations, breakdowns of retention periods into active and inactive storage periods, and many other things. Whether any of these fields has value to you depends upon your organization and your goals in utilizing the retention schedule. If your organization is in the United States, one field worth considering is a column for recording the locations or repositories where records from the various records series reside. Identifying the repositories for relevant information is a requirement for litigants under Federal Rules of Civil Procedure (F.R.C.P.) 26; so, if your organization is involved in litigation, you will have to do it anyway. Having these repositories pre-mapped on the retention schedule saves work later.

One question you will probably be faced with is whether to list individual records on the schedule beneath each records series. Such a listing is not an uncommon practice, but it has its own downsides. Before you decide, recall the earlier discussion about records lists. If you have a reasonably comprehensive list, a 200-line schedule may become a 2,000-line schedule; or, you will have cells in your tables jammed with dozens of record titles. If you're publishing an electronic schedule, you can perhaps get around this problem by using a compound document and hyperlinks, or some similar device, which also has its own issues. In any event, you will still be faced with gaps in your list, and the issue of keeping it up-to-date. If you list records as examples only, be sure that the use of examples is clearly stated in your schedule use instructions; otherwise, you will be spending time fielding inquiries from people who want to know why their particular record isn't listed.

In adding columns of information to the schedule beyond records series and retention periods, your limiting factor will eventually be lack of space. Sooner or later, you will run out of screen or out of page. Choose the additional material wisely, and limit it to things that will really help people use the retention schedule properly.

Chapter 5

Developing
Records Series

Once you've got some idea of what your structure might look like, the next question that arises is that of exactly what records series to choose. What should they be named? What should they contain? This is another area in which there is no absolute best answer. Many categories, at least at a high level, are fairly obvious, and their names are self-suggestive. Accounting and human resources records are examples of these. Every organization has them, and these names for them are both widely understood and widely used. Beyond the obvious choices, other records series will be dependent upon precisely what the organization does, and what records it has. If it manufactures things, there will be records relating to those manufacturing activities. If it's in health care, there will be records related to patient care. There's no shortcut to analyzing the activities and the records associated with them. Trying out various groupings of them until a structure is devised makes sense. In developing the series, several points to bear in mind include:

1. **Records within a series should be closely related.** The individual record types within any series will have the same retention period. Because the record types are sufficiently related, they can be treated identically for management and administrative purposes. Again, because they are used for similar purposes, they contain similar information, or they are created as part of the same process, the same retention period may apply. Regardless of the reason, the records must be sufficiently similar that no issues will arise if they are destroyed after the same period of time. If you construct a records series and discover that some of its members are being kept far, far longer than they need be, or that destruction of some of the records in the series at the end of the selected retention period is problematic, your series is probably a candidate for splitting into different series.

> Creating a general category is an invitation to place many unlike records in it, resulting in the precise sort of uncertainty that the retention schedule is supposed to avoid.

2. **Records series must be meaningful.** In order to do their job, your records series must describe actual records, with sufficient clarity to allow people to accurately decide just what records you're talking about. Not only must the series title and description be written with sufficient clarity, but also what the title and description refers to must correspond with actual, identifiable, and related records within your organization. If you can't look at a records series and describe with some accuracy the kind of records within it, it may not be a viable series. Likewise, avoid series categories such as "miscellaneous" or "general" or their many brethren. There isn't any such thing as a general record. Every record is about some particular topic and contains some particular kind of information. Creating a general category is an invitation to place many unlike records in it, resulting in the precise sort of uncertainty that the retention schedule is supposed to avoid. It's also, by the very nature of the series, impossible to assign a meaningful retention period to such a construct. A retention period assigned to a series is based upon the assumption that the records in it are reasonably similar. When the series is a "miscellaneous" series, no such assumption is warranted.

3. **Records series can have multiple uses.** By its nature, a retention schedule tells you something about your records. Large, broad records series, or "buckets," provide information about them at a very high level. Small detailed buckets provide very granular information about them. If you already have a detailed functional filing plan or plans, or an enterprise-wide indexing system, a high-level retention schedule used in conjunction with it may be all that you need. However, if you don't have these tools, your retention schedule may offer the opportunity to kill two birds with one stone. A well-developed and reasonably granular retention schedule may serve as the basis for an indexing system or filing plan. A really complex filing plan would be very much more detailed, having perhaps as many as eight or ten levels. This number is far more than are needed for most retention schedules; so, the retention schedule would, in this case, serve at the topmost three or four levels of the file plan.

Records Series Size— Little Buckets or Big Buckets?

We've discussed quite a bit about the structure of your records schedule and the need to develop sound records series. If you have already tried your hand at this, you have discovered that you can get quite detailed if you're so inclined. You could, for example, have a structure that looks something like Example 1:

Operations
    Manufacturing
        Quality Control
            Lab Testing
                Bacteriological Testing
                    Cultures
                    Wet counts
                    etc.
                Destructive Testing
                    Crush test results
                    Materials point-of-failure analysis
                    etc.
                Quantitative Analysis
                    Contaminant analysis
                    Raw materials assay
                    etc.

Example 1

That's certainly an impressive amount of detail, and if the whole schedule is as detailed, you will have very granular control of your records. However, as with most things on a retention schedule, that detail comes with a cost. Your schedule will be very long, and users will be faced with a large number of decision points whenever they classify a record. Given that the detail comes with some overhead, the question then naturally arises, is the detail necessary? Could you perhaps omit some of it and still have an effective retention schedule? The answer is, of course, "It depends." Although the detail comes with some overhead, so does omission of the detail. Therefore, you need to make some decisions about your overall goals in order to determine how much detail, and where, is necessary in order to support those goals with a minimum of overhead. We began that discussion above. Now let's look at the subject in a bit more detail.

Why Worry About Bucket Size?

In order to decide how much detail you need, you need to understand how the detail, or lack of it, affects the schedule and your use of it. Consider Example 1. If the records in question relate to the manufacture of a heavily regulated and extensively tested product, such as pharmaceuticals or medical

> You need to understand how the detail, or lack of it, affects the schedule and your use of it.

devices, a great many different quality control records may apply, and those records will be subject to extensive legal regulation, including records retention requirements. Because many of the records relate to a particular batch of product or to an individual medical device, they will also be very voluminous, which creates a certain tension. On one hand, maintaining the records for the correct length of time is very important. If a government inspection occurs and the required records are not available, the consequences are likely to be severe. On the other hand, the volumes of records make them costly to manage, and if poorly managed, difficult to find in the event that a government inspection occurs.

If legal and operational requirements combine to impose different retention periods on the various kinds of quality control records, these conflicting demands can be met by a granular listing like the one in Example 1. The result might look something like Example 2:

Operations
    Manufacturing
        Quality Control
            Lab Testing
                Bacteriological Testing   3 years
                Destructive Testing   5 years
                Quantitative Analysis   8 years

Example 2

On the other hand, suppose that all lab testing records have a retention period of five years. In that case, the structure can be simplified to something like Example 3:

Operations
    Manufacturing
        Quality Control
            Lab Testing   5 years

Example 3

Suppose further that all quality control records, including records other than lab testing records, also have a five-year retention period. The structure could be simplified still more, to something like Example 4:

Operations
    Manufacturing
        Quality Control   5 years

Example 4

Now, suppose that once again, the records have different retention periods, as in Example 2, but that you are willing to live with a longer-than-the-minimum retention period for some of them. The structure of Example 1 could be simplified like the following in Example 5:

    Operations
        Manufacturing
            Quality Control
                Lab Testing   8 years

Example 5

Now, suppose still further that some other quality control record has a ten-year retention period, but once again, you are willing to live with it for all your quality control records, taking into account extra storage costs, additional records to be produced during audits, and so on. In that case, the structure can be simplified to something like Example 6:

    Operations
        Manufacturing
            Quality Control   10 years

Example 6

These examples illustrate the tradeoffs between small and narrowly tailored buckets and larger, more inclusive buckets. In Example 2, the schedule shows maximum detail, and retention periods have been reduced as much as business needs and legal requirements permit. The cost, including this detail, is that the complete retention schedule is likely to be quite long and complex. Other costs flow from this detail as well: configuring an electronic records management system to use this schedule will be a relatively complex task, and user training must be more thorough if users are to apply the schedule correctly.

Example 6 is at the opposite end of the spectrum. The structure has been simplified as much as possible by lumping a great many records into a single "Quality Control" bucket; and if the rest of the schedule has been similarly simplified, the length and complexity of the whole schedule is undoubtedly reduced dramatically. This simplified structure in turn means simplified software configuration, simpler user training, and so on. On the down side, however, the "Quality Control" bucket tells you nothing about what kinds of quality control records you actually have; so, you had better be able to get this information somewhere else, or you will be in trouble when that government inspector shows up. In addition, you are now stuck with a 10-year retention period for all quality control records, even though many could have much shorter retention periods. That extra retention time equates to keeping around a lot of dead wood for a long time, which means a variety of additional costs, including storing, finding, and producing additional records during inspections, investigations, and lawsuits.

The other examples show some intermediate outcomes from moving from narrowly tailored buckets to larger catch-all buckets. In Example 3, you didn't lengthen any retention periods, but you lost a lot of detail about your records. In Example 4, you have again not lengthened any retention periods, but you have lost still more detail. In Example 5 you lost detail and lengthened retention periods, but not to the extent shown in Example 6.

The Tradeoffs

In each case, the simplification may result in some advantages in configuration and training, but it may also result in some increased costs for storage, retrieval, and other management activities. If differing retention periods are involved in the nesting of the buckets, the retention periods for many records get longer. This result is unavoidable. Not only does the larger bucket scoop up records, it also scoops up their retention periods. Remember, each smaller bucket had or would have had some sort of retention period that was attached to it for operational or legal reasons. These retention periods can't be ignored when scooping up the smaller buckets into larger ones. The same laws still apply, and the same operational needs still exist; and they follow the record into the larger bucket. Because the larger bucket can have only one retention period, the longest retention period applicable to anything in the bucket gets applied to everything in the bucket.

> Reducing retention periods to minimums will necessarily entail breaking up large buckets so as to be able to reduce retention periods for some member of the buckets.

Balancing the Factors

Developing an optimal solution to this problem is not possible. An optimal solution for any one factor necessarily means a very suboptimal solution for one or more of the other factors. Larger buckets, for example, conflict with minimizing retention periods. The larger your buckets, the more conservative your retention periods will be. Reducing retention periods to minimums will necessarily entail breaking up large buckets so as to be able to reduce retention periods for some member of the buckets. You can't avoid this conflict. When developing your records series (your buckets), your goal is to achieve the best possible balance between these competing factors, minimizing insofar as possible the worst effects of each factor and maximizing those factors that are most desirable or necessary for your organization.

Other factors may influence the decisions you make. For example, suppose that, using the examples above, your organization already has a detailed records index for its manufacturing and quality control records, and that therefore, lack of detail on the retention schedule is not a concern. If, as in Example 4, all quality control records have a retention period of five years, a simple retention schedule could be mapped to a complex records index on a many-to-one basis, like shown in Example 7:

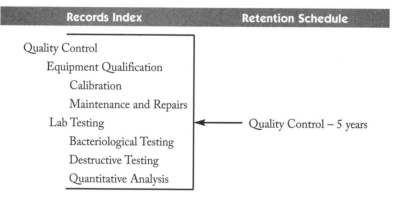

Example 7

Even if retention periods for some of these records could possibly be less than five years, you can do the same mapping if you are willing to live with whatever downside comes with the longer retention periods that result. You could, of course, also take any one of several other courses, applying one retention period to Lab Testing, another to Equipment Qualification, and so on, or applying retention periods at the most granular level available, even breaking down Lab Testing into its component parts if differing retention periods made doing so worthwhile.

Problematic Situations

Some repositories can't be broken down into constituent parts for retention purposes. For example, the general ledger system of a company might reside in a single large software installation. Although reports can be run that simulate all traditional accounting records, the data set underlying them may be a single interlinked data set that can't be parsed out into a "ledger," "journal," and so on. In this case, like it or not, your records series is "Accounting System," or some such thing, and its retention period is the longest one applicable to any individual traditional accounting record.

Some hybrid situations may also exist. For example, the company could run a general ledger software package, and it could also receive paper and electronic invoices from vendors that are managed separately from the electronic accounting system. If, as is possible, the invoices can be assigned a shorter retention period than the general ledger system, it might be worthwhile to have a single large bucket for the "Accounting System" and a smaller, narrow bucket for vendor invoices. In some situations, this big-bucket-with-an-exception approach may be the only way to make a big bucket approach work. One such case is when one potential member of the big bucket is subject to a legally imposed maximum retention period, a situation commonly seen in Europe. If the bigger bucket would result in extending this period, it's either big-bucket-with-an-exception or small buckets if you don't want to violate the law. In other cases, one potential member of the big bucket has a mandatory retention period so far out of line with the other members that including it would impose unreasonable or impossible burdens on someone. Again, it's either big-bucket-with-an-exception or small buckets.

This hybrid situation points to an important fact: you don't necessarily need to go "big bucket" or "small bucket." You can instead tailor your bucket sizes to what is realistically possible, or to accommodate needed exceptions to what is an otherwise reasonable rule, but into which a particular record type cannot be forced without also forcing an unreasonable or illegal retention period. That more realistic retention schedule can include a mixture of large and small buckets as the situation demands.

> Tailor your bucket sizes to what is realistically possible, or to accommodate needed exceptions to what is an otherwise reasonable rule, but into which a particular record type cannot be forced without also forcing an unreasonable or illegal retention period.

Building Big Buckets

You cannot create just any old buckets you want, so as to get any retention periods you feel like, and wind up with a small handful of nice big buckets. You might, for example, be tempted to look at a number of records that all potentially have five-year retention periods, say a group like this one in Example 8:

Lab Testing
Internal Reporting
Hazardous Waste Manifests
Motor Overhauls
Customs Manifests
etc.
etc.

Example 8

You might try to lump them into a single big bucket. "That" you might say, "would kill a lot of birds with one stone. All these records that make for a lot of messy complexity on the schedule get dealt with in one fell swoop." If you followed through on that thought and created the bucket, it would be a bad idea. If you think back to the previous discussions on structure and indexing, it will quickly become clear that such a bucket would violate most of the rules, and would not be very helpful to users. The records are completely unrelated functionally and are governed by a broad hodgepodge of laws, risk management considerations, and business requirements.

Consequently, trying to fit such a bucket into a retention schedule poses a number of problems that will inevitably yield poor solutions: First, where would you place the bucket on the schedule? Then, what would you call it? General? Miscellaneous? Various? And then, when someone tried to use the schedule, how would they know what records series they were looking for without reading what would necessarily be a long and very detailed description? Worse, what if someone needed to classify a record not explicitly listed on the schedule? Such a miscellaneous, catch-all bucket is sure to invite confusion, and with it, misclassification of the record. The confusion and misclassification will defeat everything discussed so far about structures and indexing, and ultimately about the ease and accuracy with which personnel will use the schedule. Defeating these principles is a bad thing, and it will create far more problems than are solved by creating such a patchwork bucket, regardless of—or perhaps more accurately, in proportion to—how many records you managed to sweep into your bucket.

Nesting Buckets

Think of bigger buckets as being rather like those nesting Russian dolls. If you have a big set of them, you can get quite a few smaller ones into the biggest one, and they all fit snugly within each other. But, and it's a big but, it only works if the smaller dolls are part of the same set as the larger ones. If you try to put in other dolls, they won't fit nicely, limbs or clothing will stick out, and the dolls won't close up correctly.

Likewise with records series and buckets, the little buckets you nest up into bigger buckets must all be from the same "set"—the same topic on the retention schedule. Instead of smaller dolls, you have subseries and sub-subseries. When you go big bucket, you nest them up, scooping up several sub-subseries into one subseries, several subseries into one series, and so on until you have a bucket size that suits your organization. If you have done it right, everything nests up nicely and snugly. If you do it wrong and try to include things that don't belong there, you will have bits sticking out here and there, and the thing won't nest up properly or close up correctly, just like the Russian doll.

This discussion should point to the fact that bigger buckets aren't a substitute for knowing about your records in detail, or a labor-saving shortcut when developing your retention schedule. To the contrary, if you're going to do it right, going big bucket involves some extra steps. In order to know what little buckets you can nest up, you must first know what little buckets you have, and what the retention consequences of nesting them up will be. You first have to build out a detailed schedule, including retention periods; and then, after you've completed this structure, you can analyze it for opportunities to nest things up. Then you recalculate retention periods and see if you can live with the consequences. If you can't, you then have to determine whether alternative strategies will work—medium-size buckets, big buckets, and some little-bucket exceptions; or perhaps a combination of all these sizes. After some tinkering around, you eventually arrive at some combination of buckets that gets the job done. If you had stuck with small buckets, you would have been done long ago.

Considering Real-World Consequences

As you're doing that analysis, bear in mind the real-world consequences of what you're doing. Some kinds of records are generated in massive quantities (for example, many kinds of low-level production records), and others are stored in a manner that imposes real physical constraints on the number of records that can be stored (for example, records stored in machine buffers with finite and unchangeable capacities). Changing a retention number on a schedule from 1 year to 10 years is simple to do, because you've nested some records series up into a bigger bucket. However, doing so may place someone in the situation of incurring massive costs or difficulties to comply, or even make compliance impossible. Therefore, make very sure that the people who must live with your big-bucket retention periods are willing and able to do so. If they can't or won't, its back to the drawing board.

The Retention Schedule as an Index

The use of big buckets on a retention schedule assumes that you have some other method of classifying and retrieving records. That method could be a file plan, an index, an electronic data structure, or something else. In this case, the retention schedule isn't really serving as an index. Instead, it's a secondary structure that piggybacks onto whatever other data structure you're using.

On the other hand, you may find that your organization has no systematic classification tool for its records in place and nothing to piggyback onto. Your retention schedule may in that case represent the only formal, global classification of the organization's records that exists. It may therefore wind up as the de facto file plan for the organization. That's not a bad thing. To the contrary, if there's no file plan or data structure in place, the retention schedule's ability to serve as one may prove a welcome improvement in the organization's ability to manage its records.

If, however, you do not have a file plan or data structure in place, you may find that bigger buckets aren't the solution for you. For categorization and search and retrieval purposes, a single large category called "Quality Control" isn't much help. Much more useful is something along the lines of Example 1 on page 47, where the various quality control records are broken out in some detail. If you go this route, the process and analysis don't change—you still have to categorize and organize your records into a meaningful structure. The outcome, however, can be quite different, and in a sense, you move in the opposite direction. Rather than looking to nest up records series into bigger buckets, you may be looking for rational ways to break them into smaller buckets that serve to identify discrete records sets.

If you do this, you may wind up with several similar records series with the same retention period, something like this:

Contracts

Asset purchase and sale	Contract Life + 6 years
Confidentiality agreements	Contract Life + 6 years
Leases	Contract Life + 6 years
Real estate contracts	Contract Life + 6 years
Vendor contracts	Contract Life + 6 years

That's okay. Analytically, this situation is much like that in Example 6. There is in effect a single retention category, "Contracts," being applied to a number of document types. On the other hand, if you extended this list to include other kinds of contracts, it's also entirely possible that you would also wind up with some different retention periods as well. This level of detail allows you to deal with those other retention periods with ease. Thus, a high degree of granularity also provides the maximum flexibility in assigning retention periods, and the maximum opportunity to reduce retention periods to the shortest minimums.

Deciding on Bucket Size

As you can see, there's no best bucket size. In the right situation, big buckets will work just fine, but in other situations, small and detailed buckets are best. In still other situations, medium buckets, or a mix of large and small, may work best. You can only know what bucket size or mix of bucket sizes is best if you know a great deal about your records, have a good sense of how your retention schedule will be used and what it will be used for, and what other tools—file plans, indices, and data structures—will be used in conjunction with it. Once you understand where you are and where you intend to go, you can develop a structure, including whatever bucket size you decide upon, that will support that goal.

Building Your Structure and Index

When you're ready to start building a retention schedule structure, you will be faced with several questions about what to call your records series, how to arrange them, and in what order to put them. The answers to these questions are important—a well-devised structure will be user-friendly and achieve good results. A poor structure will discourage use and lead to poor classification decisions. Therefore, investing the time to choose good terms and to rank and order them in a way that assists users in finding records is worthwhile. The next chapter covers some of these details and describes how to go about building a structure that will guide users to the right place on the schedule.

Chapter 6

Detailed Considerations in Building and Naming Records Series

The discussion of building a structure for your records retention schedule began in previous chapters. Because the structure of the records retention schedule guides users through the schedule, getting it right is worth the effort. How can you build the structure for the retention schedule and describe its contents so that you achieve maximum clarity and usability?

The structure is a kind of index, and an index is a way of ordering and distilling information. Whatever you are indexing—records in a retention schedule, topics in a book, or kinds of trees in New Hampshire—the goal is always the same: to take a large body of information, extract the essential points, and place those essentials into a sequence and into categories that make sense to readers. They should then be able to find the particular points of information that they are interested in by moving from general topics to more precise topics. The structure of a retention schedule should work in the same way. After all, if users can't find a record, they can't find its retention period. Your goal is to help users find first the record, then its retention period. Secondarily, you may want to help them find other information, but these two points are primary.

If your organization is large, you could have a great many records, which could mean an awful lot of looking if things aren't well-organized. That lack of organization tells you another thing about an index: if the subject matter is voluminous, one goal of the index must be to reduce the amount of time spent searching. Not only should your index permit users to find things, it should also help them find things quickly and with a minimum of confusion. How can this outcome be accomplished?

If the subject matter is voluminous, one goal of the index must be to reduce the amount of time spent searching.

Index Logic

When constructing an index, you're trying to take a series of topics—in this case, record types—and place them into some order that gets users rapidly from the most general of all situations—just starting—to the most detailed level of information that your index provides. If they are to do that, each topic and subtopic must serve as a guidepost. As users scan it, they should be able to either accept it as relevant and consider its subtopics, or reject it as irrelevant and proceed to the next topic. Consider as an example a simple tiered index like the following:

　　Accounting
　　　　Accounts payable
　　　　Accounts receivable
　　Human resources
　　　　Benefits files
　　　　Personnel files

This structure employs a system of logic—each kind of record on an interior level is a subtype of the record type found on the first level. Assuming that you follow through consistently with this logic, you are making life easier for your users. They can confidently scan through the first levels and select the one of interest, say human resources, without worrying that they have missed a human resources record of interest because it's located somewhere else. If the schedule is complex, you might add a third level of detail. Again, the goal is the same—having identified a level and sublevel, users can then peruse the sub-subtopics with a high degree of confidence that they are looking in the right place. In fact, the larger and more complex the schedule, the more important this confidence becomes. If the schedule is not well done, you will have many more opportunities for false starts and incorrect choices, and as a result, users will waste much more time browsing through the schedule hoping to hit upon the correct spot.

As you take your records listings, interview notes, and survey forms in hand, and begin analyzing your results, you should consider the logic that you will use in the structure of the schedule. One already pointed out obvious consideration is that the schedule must go from the general to the specific. Beyond that, however, it should do so in a way—or perhaps more precisely, on a path—that makes sense to users. If you are developing a pure departmental schedule, doing so may be a straightforward exercise in working from an org chart:

The schedule must go from the general to the specific.

Administration
 Facilities
  Office layout
  Work orders

and so on

On the other hand, if you are developing a functional retention schedule, you will need to give some thought to how every record or record type that your data gathering efforts turned up fits into some overall scheme of logic. Even if you are developing a departmental retention schedule, in complex departments or departments with many record types, you will probably still need some sort of structure for organizing the records.

Consequently, you need to think about what each record is for and what job it *does* within the organization. You, like your users, must work from the general to the specific: is it a financial record of some type? If so, is it accounting? Pure finance? Tax perhaps? Payables? Receivables? Depreciation?

Your goal is to take your mass of records and sort it into piles of records that are related in some way that is intuitive and meaningful to you, and hopefully will be to your users as well. Then, you take each pile, and break it down into a series of smaller piles, and these piles into still smaller piles, and so on to the level of detail that you're seeking. Taking this process to its end point, you will eventually arrive at individual record titles. Each pile that you have created represents a records series; and all but the first set of large piles are subseries of something else.

On the higher levels of your index, the breakdowns will often be fairly obvious, if (and only if) you know enough about the functional uses of the records you have captured—accounting, human resources, manufacturing, environmental, and other records that fall within broad categories. Within those broad categories, however, you will need to think a little harder about your logic. If your company manufactures complex or highly regulated products, such as airplanes or medical devices, you will discover that a vast number of records are associated with the manufacturing process, from design to testing to certification to manufacture to post-production monitoring. Plopping them all into a gigantic "products manufacturing" bucket may not be a suitable solution, nor may leaving them as a very long list of complex records titles. Even if you're with the pizza company discussed in Chapter 4, you will discover that the pizza factory has a surprisingly large variety of manufacturing, product testing, engineering, and other records.

At this point, you need to think very hard about the logical boundaries of any categories you create, if you are to avoid confounding users. You will need to delve into the processes themselves, so as to gain an understanding of what each record does. As in the airplane manufacturing example, that delving might mean subtopics such as design records, build records, quality control and testing, and so on. As with the simpler examples, the same logic should control the design—each topic should completely subsume its subtopics, and the subtopics shouldn't "leak" from one topic into other topics if it can be avoided. Otherwise, users will be confused and waste their time. Stopping leakage is particularly important if you are planning to map the retention schedule to a pre-existing record plan or index. Records series that are not well-bounded will cause problems during the mapping, because there won't be a straightforward relationship between the records series and the record plan.

Terminology

A second important point about indexing is choice of terminology. Your index is a sort of street map, and every term in it is a street sign that is supposed to tell users whether to turn down that street or go to the next one. Both the road system and the street signs that mark it should take users smoothly from the arterials to the boulevards to the back streets and finally to the address they are seeking. Users can only navigate the route correctly and with confidence if the information on each street sign is clear and informative. Every topic and subtopic, and every description, should be selected carefully to accomplish this goal. At its most obvious, avoid meaningless topics such as "general" or "miscellaneous." Such terms tell the user nothing at all about what kind of records you may have included within the category.

Likewise, describing records as "reports" or "correspondence" is equally valueless. What sort of reports are you talking about? Reports or correspondence on the monthly desk supplies inventory will have a far different retention period than reports and correspondence on an oil refinery explosion. You certainly don't want to co-mingle or confuse the records categories, but if all your schedule shows is "reports," that is exactly what you're inviting, and whatever retention period you choose will be considerably out of line for some records that wind up in that category.

Of course, you may know perfectly well what kinds of reports and correspondence you are have included, and your chosen retention period may line up perfectly with the records you have in mind. Unfortunately, users cannot read your mind when they're consulting the retention schedule. All they have to go by are the words you placed onto the page. You must therefore choose words that adequately describe whatever it is you had in mind and that give your users a high degree of confidence that the choices they make are the ones you intended them to make.

Fortunately, this trap can be avoided. Most of the processes that the records document are well-understood and have commonly understood names and descriptors—*if* you have taken the trouble to really understand your organization and its processes. This is often where you have the opportunity to gauge the adequacy of your data collection and analysis. If you have a group of records that you cannot index with confidence, you probably don't understand the process that they document as well as you need to. You need to find out what those records do before you index them. Likewise, if you know what the process is but can't find a short, clear functional descriptor for it that captures the records you have uncovered, you probably don't understand the records or the process they support well enough, and again, you probably need to do a bit more homework.

You may find that many departments in your organization are acronym-driven, or that particular records or records series have informal names that are commonly used. If so, using these terms on the retention schedule is tempting. It's wise, however, to be cautious in using acronyms or informal names on records series. They may be acceptable and informative if universally understood and used (for example, OSHA for Occupational Safety and Health Administration); but in other cases, they may confuse personnel outside the particular department that uses the term, leaving them wondering just what a Blue Book or a BOMA might be.

Another factor to consider in naming records series is length. Remember, readers will in many cases be scanning the schedule for items of interest, or in order to analyze how it's constructed. The longer the names of your records series, the harder scanning it will be to do efficiently. Your job is to choose records series titles that effectively convey the information users need about the series in a small handful of words—ideally, as few as two or three. If you must use more, your goal is then to place the more important terms to the left. This way, readers can effectively scan the beginning of each entry for relevance without having to read the entire entry before making a decision.

> Your job is to choose records series titles that effectively convey the information users need about the series in a small handful of words—ideally, as few as two or three.

Descriptions

Records series titles are often accompanied by descriptions. These handy aids can be used very effectively to clear up any lingering ambiguity that your choice of series titles or topics couldn't eliminate. Your descriptions should take up where the record series title left off, and give the reader a clear and detailed picture of exactly the kind of records to be found in the series. The description expands upon the title to explain to the user exactly what kind of records the series contains. Once again, your goals are clarity and certainty. If you don't achieve them, your descriptions are just more clutter on the page.

Descriptions may in some cases seem unnecessary. Most people know, for example, what personnel files are and what they are called. In less obvious cases however, they may be important classification aids. In all cases, you should be mindful that beginners will always appreciate a tightly drafted and informative description.

On the other hand, the description is another point at which clarity and certainty are competing with other factors. Your readers may be perusing a number of records series; therefore, they will have to read a number of descriptions. If each one is a long block of dense and turgid text, users are not encouraged to read them carefully and thoroughly, and they will remain uninformed, regardless of the information contained in the text that they have skipped. As a practical matter, records series descriptions will get only a small allotment of space on the retention schedule. As a result, if you are unable to craft a really succinct and informative description of a sentence or two, you will wind up with descriptions in a microscopic font, spreadsheet rows or columns that each take up half the screen, or some other problem that impairs the usability of your retention schedule generally and of the descriptions in particular.

Therefore, write, write, write, to get your descriptions as informative as they need to be, and then edit, edit, edit, to get them down to a reasonable length based upon your space limitations, your judgment of what length readers will tolerate, and your editorial judgment of how much they really need. With practice, and in combination with well-chosen and well-crafted topics and records series titles, you will be able to get most descriptions down to a reasonable length without unduly impairing their descriptive value.

> The description expands upon the title to explain to the user exactly what kind of records the series contains.

Putting It All Together

To see how this process works, consider the development of a records series on financial compliance audits. As a first stab, you might pick a series title called:

Records and Documents Related to Audits and Other Activities Arising from Sarbanes-Oxley and Similar Matters

This title violates several rules: it is too long; the first few words are not particularly informative—because it is a records retention schedule, users have probably already figured out that records and documents are involved; and it is vague overall. Individuals from other countries (and even American users) may have no idea what Sarbanes-Oxley is; and if so, they will also have no idea what kinds of "Other Activities" or "Similar Matters" may be involved. Imagine a retention schedule with two or three hundred series titles like this one, and you can begin to picture the difficulties your readers will face when trying to locate what they need. So, take a second stab at it, using a description to help.

Records Series	Description
Sarbanes-Oxley Records	Records of Sarbanes-Oxley activities

This example isn't much better. The records series title still tells you little or nothing about what kind of records might be found in the series unless you are familiar with the Sarbanes-Oxley Act and what it entails. Worse, the whole construction is recursive. When you refer to the description for clarification, none is to be found. It simply repeats the records series title, and leaves the reader in the dark about what kind of records and what they do. Even if users know what the Sarbanes-Oxley Act is, they may not have any idea of what records it might generate, and this description certainly doesn't tell them. So, recast the description:

Records Series	Description
Sarbanes-Oxley Records	Records, reports, documents, work papers, and other content, whether in paper, electronic, or microfilm, in any location, documenting audits, inspections, analysis, and any other activity conducted pursuant to or in furtherance of the application of the Sarbanes-Oxley Act of 2002 or any regulation or subsidiary legislation enacted or promulgated thereto; and including any analysis of executive compliance or other matters that may impact corporate compliance.

Better—at least users now know something about what kind of records are in the series. On the other hand, the description is a bit of a handful. Users may have gotten the gist of the description about halfway through; the rest is just taking up space. They may still be uncertain about just exactly what Sarbanes-Oxley is all about; they know that it's about audits, but what kind?

Try again, and consider the same records series recast into a reasonable structure and supported by a clear and succinct description:

Records Series 1 Records Series 2	Description
Financial Compliance and Audits	
Sarbanes-Oxley audits	Audit reports and supporting work papers documenting audits establishing the adequacy of financial and accounting controls per the Sarbanes-Oxley Act.

This combination of records series and description clarifies things considerably. Users now know that Sarbanes-Oxley records are a species of financial compliance records and that they consist of audit reports and supporting work papers. The structure also allows you to deal with the "Similar Matters" mentioned earlier in a similar manner, thus:

Records Series 1 Records Series 2	Description
Financial Compliance and Audits	
Payroll Audits	Audit reports and work papers documenting results of audits of payroll records for compliance with provincial, state and federal wage, tax, and withholding laws.
Sarbanes-Oxley Audits	Audit reports and supporting work papers documenting audits establishing the adequacy of financial and accounting controls per the Sarbanes-Oxley Act.
Securities Compliance Audits	Audit reports and work papers documenting compliance with rules regarding the offering of stock, shareholder matters and other matters related to stock issuance and ownership.

If you take the time to build logic and clarity into your retention schedule, the result will be much more useful to your organization than one that is haphazardly put together.

As you work through your retention schedule building the structure, this sort of logic and clarity should be your ongoing goal. If you take the time to build logic and clarity into your retention schedule, the result will be much more useful to your organization than one that is haphazardly put together.

Making Choices and Arbitrary Decisions

When creating your retention schedule, you will be faced with situations in which more than one option for a structure or grouping is available. You could, for example, place "Tax" as a subseries under "Accounting and Finance," or you could rank it at the same level as accounting or finance. Likewise, you could create a series containing all finance and audits, or you could place tax audits as a subseries under Tax. There are many other places on the typical records retention schedule where similar choices can be made. The Sarbanes-Oxley example above could be done any of several other ways.

No one best solution is available in these cases. In some cases, the choice will be driven by how the records are maintained or what they are used for. In other cases, some logic or other reason will be the most appealing or intuitive. In still other cases, the decision will come down to an arbitrary choice between equally good structures. That's okay. Any index is to some extent a guessing game between the indexer and user, and there's always a learning curve as users become familiar with the logic employed by the indexer and the resulting data structure. When in doubt, experiment with different combinations, and get some feedback from your users. Eventually, you will arrive at a combination that is the most satisfactory for your organization; but if it comes down to your judgment call, don't be afraid to exercise that judgment.

Additional Possibilities

So far, the discussion has been about indexing and structure in the traditional tiered structure of a written, paper-based index. There's certainly nothing wrong with this structure—the tiered display of topic, subtopic, and so on is easy to construct, and it is both intuitive and easy to read. Today, however, additional options and choices are available. Even on a simple spreadsheet, a suitably constructed schedule can be resorted and massaged to rearrange the structure in a number of different ways; and, if the retention schedule resides in a database, such as records management software of some type, many additional options may be available.

First and foremost, in a database format, you're not limited to the single, tiered display. The data elements in the retention schedule index can be filtered, rearranged, sorted, and displayed in a potentially large variety of ways. Further, database residence for your retention schedule may also permit the inclusion of keywords, departmental assignments and other attributes for each records series. You could of course, also include these things on a paper-based schedule, but in a database environment, they become far more powerful and useful tools, because they are now searchable and otherwise subject to manipulation.

The relational power of the database allows you to look at your data in any form or order you choose (that is supported by your database, of course), without losing any relationships between records series and subseries, assignments of records to series, or other data relationships. It also allows you to map your retention schedule to an existing file plan or data structure, or if there is no existing data structure, to use your retention schedule as the basis for one.

Of course, to accomplish this plan, your retention schedule must be compatible with the capabilities of the software within which it will reside. There's no point in having a three-deep index if your software will support only two levels of indexing. Worse, if your data structure really needs that third level to be useful, you may find that importing a three-deep structure into a software product that supports only a two-deep index has gutted your retention schedule, and you will have to rework it. Likewise, you may have field length, field type, or other restrictions that require you to edit your schedule.

On the other hand, your software may have capabilities that you haven't considered, such as keyword fields and similar features that are really useful, as well as versatile and powerful search and filtering capabilities. In the best case, this situation allows the best of both worlds: you can view and use your retention schedule in traditional tiered index format if that suits you, but you can also squash down your index and query interior levels without going through the top level, while simultaneously adding keywords and other parameters to the search or filter. These capabilities can produce powerful results if properly deployed. If you're going to take advantage of these capabilities, you may have to consciously build your retention schedule to do so. You may need to flesh out additional data fields by building keyword lists and other aids.

If you are building a retention schedule for use with a particular software product, it's a good idea to study the product in question and determine its capabilities prior to developing the schedule. This way, you can make sure that you are taking maximum advantage of its capabilities with a minimum of reworking of your retention schedule. If you're contemplating putting your retention schedule into a database or records management software package at some later time but have not yet chosen the particular software, build it in a flexible format, such as a spreadsheet, that can easily be manipulated and augmented so as to give yourself some flexibility to accommodate whatever software is chosen. If someone is programming a custom product to support your retention schedule, work closely with them during the design and development of the product; otherwise you may be disappointed with your custom product.

The Need for Clarity

Remember, clarity, and informing and guiding users are your foremost considerations in building an indexing structure. Not only must the structure and terms used clearly inform users of the kinds of records you are talking about, but when they've followed the path provided by your index to its end, actual, identifiable records must be at the end of it, and they must be the ones you intended to be there. It's easy to fall in love with your own terminology, or with a particular indexing logic, and lose sight of the fact that your users weren't inside your head when you conceived your terms and logic, and they aren't as familiar with either the records or the retention schedule as you are.

Make sure that the structure you build is meaningful to your users. They are the ones that count. If that means sacrificing the theoretical purity of your structure's logic, or choosing layman's terms instead of the technical terms you might prefer, don't hesitate to do so. The retention schedule is a tool, and tools are meant to be used. An elegantly finished but impractical tool may look nice, but the one that gets used is the utilitarian one, designed to get the job done.

Make sure that the structure you build is meaningful to your users. They are the ones that count.

Chapter 7

Deriving
Retention Periods

Thus far, we've taken retention periods for granted, without much discussion of exactly how a retention period for a record is determined. Now it's time to consider retention periods in more detail. The retention period for a record is derived from one of several factors, or a combination of factors. The typical factors for most organizations are support of active business processes, legal requirements, risk management concerns, and evidentiary needs. For some organizations, research, trending and analysis, and the need or desire to maintain records for historical or cultural preservation purposes may also be important. For governmental entities, a variety of other issues, from open records laws to the government's role as repository of important, long-term documents, such as deeds, may also factor into the mix. Before looking at how the retention period is determined, first consider those factors and how they affect overall retention periods.

Support of Business Processes

In the records retention business, it's sometimes possible to be blind to the fact that most of the records created are created to support business processes. In the rush to get rid of records as quickly as possible, it's easy to forget that someone in the organization actually needs them to get some work done—why they were created in the first place. If the records are gone before that work is done, someone's work has been made a lot harder, and maybe impossible. In the process, the ability of the organization to accomplish whatever it does is impaired—

whether that something is to turn a profit for shareholders, make a scientific discovery, or support a missionary in Africa. Obviously, that's not a good idea.

The business needs that records support, and the time period for which the process needs the record, will vary widely by business process and record type. For accounting records, they are needed to pay the bills and determine whether the organization is making money. For warehousing records, the purpose is to locate supplies and raw materials and deliver them to the factory floor. For personnel records, they are used to ensure that managers are managing employees effectively and treating them fairly. In these and all the many other situations you will encounter in the typical organization, there's no substitute for learning about the business process, the records created in support of it, and what those records are used for.

An important thing to remember about business need in support of an active process is that it's generally, but not always, a finite need. The bill gets paid, the supplies get delivered and used, and the employee retires. Eventually, the record's role in supporting the business process is completed, and if no other uses for the record are in the mix of retention factors, the record is eligible for destruction. For many records, this determination occurs relatively quickly. Often, within a year or two of its creation, the use of a record in support of active business processes is concluded, and further retention of the record, if any, is based upon other factors. However, in many cases, the period of active use can be longer, sometimes much longer. In this example, the bill will probably be paid within a month or two and any billing disputes resolved in under a year. On the other hand, for tax purposes, the same record might have a life of ten years or so. A personnel file might well have an active life of decades if the employee is long-term. Records related to the negotiation of a labor contract may have a useful life of decades. In the case of an engineering or architectural document for a building, that period could extend to the life of the building, potentially a very long time indeed. As with so many other things on a retention schedule, the length of the period of business need is something that can't be determined in a vacuum. You need to know what your records are used for, and why, and ultimately, for how long.

> The length of the period of business need is something that can't be determined in a vacuum. You need to know what your records are used for, and why, and ultimately, for how long.

Legal Requirements

Legal requirements are also a fact of life for many records. Although a great many records are not subject to explicit legal requirements, many are. The range is broad and dependent upon the industry and the activities the organization undertakes. Even a small organization in an unregulated industry will be subject to tax requirements that affect its accounting records, and human resources laws that affect its personnel and payroll records. On the other end of the scale, large organizations in heavily regulated industries will also find themselves subject to a wide range of environmental laws, workplace safety regulations, and requirements specific to the products or processes of that industry. In heavily regulated industries, particularly where safety is a concern, the level of regulation can be both extensive and minute, with precise and detailed requirements detailing exactly what information must be recorded, the form in which it must be recorded, and explicit and detailed retention periods, often coupled with onerous penalties for failure to maintain the records properly.

Although most legal requirements affecting records retention impose minimum retention periods, with no penalty for retaining records longer, increasingly the situation is that legal requirements impose *maximum* retention periods, beyond which a record cannot legally be retained. Generally, these requirements affect personal information of some sort such as medical records, personal financial information, and so on. These requirements are becoming common in Europe, but they are not unknown in the United States. Sometimes, as with the American Health Insurance Portability and Accountability Act (HIPAA) or the European Union Data Privacy Directive, the requirement is a vague "keep-the-record-only-as-long-as-needed-for-the-original-purpose" requirement. However, increasingly, the maximum period is set forth as an explicit, sometimes very short, period. If you are contemplating going big bucket on your retention schedule, it's worth bearing in mind the potential applicability of any maximum retention periods. They will affect your ability to nest up your buckets and may drive some of the structure of your schedule.

Another important thing to bear in mind about legal requirements is that they come from many different sources, and often overlap or impose different requirements. It's annoying to find out that your state or province has four different agencies that impose a retention requirement on your payroll records, and that they aren't the same; but it's often a fact of life. Multiply that by 50 states, or 13 provinces and territories, or 50 countries, and you have a lot of people with a finger in your payroll records. Additionally, if the wage and hour agency has a three-year retention period but the unemployment compensation agency has a six-year period, you're stuck with six. You can't just ignore the unemployment compensation folks because the wage and hour people say something different and that you like better. Both requirements have the force of law, and both agencies have enforcement power for their requirements.

The situation can get worse. Those same payroll records also have general tax implications, so you've now got an assortment of income tax laws involved, and maybe some general requirements for accounting records just to round things out. To top things off, the personal data in those payroll records may be subject to some privacy law. The result of all is that you may be faced with a number of different legal requirements that are applicable to a single record or record type. The larger your buckets, the worse this problem becomes, as your larger buckets capture broader and broader classes of records, along with their associated legal requirements.

On the other hand, you can go overboard in applying legal requirements to records. Most requirements apply to a specific and relatively narrow class of record. It's tempting to shortcut things and apply some requirement to some large chunk of your records rather than taking the time to parse out exactly what requirements apply to what records, but doing so will likely result in applying the requirement to many records that are not subject to it. That in turn can result in needlessly long retention periods, often considerably longer than necessary. If you're going to go big bucket this is one more reason to go granular first, and then nest up the buckets after you have a good understanding of exactly what's being nested up and what the consequences are.

Risk Management and Evidence

Although most of an organization's records are created to support a business process, some are not. Many environmental monitoring records are examples. A legal requirement demands their creation as an evidentiary and audit trail to ensure that an environmentally sensitive activity, such as discharging pollutants from a smokestack, is being carried out in an acceptable manner. Other records serve a dual business and evidentiary purpose. Accounting records, for example, are created to permit organizations to manage the financial aspects of their business, but also to serve the very important role of demonstrating tax compliance. Of course, virtually any records could end up as evidence in a lawsuit or investigation.

Records created specifically in response to a legally mandated audit trail requirement often have a required retention period. However, many other records that may wind up as evidence do not, and even for those that do have a legal retention period, there is at least a possibility that the need to retain them as evidence will outlast the statutory retention period, as well as any business need for the records. When this situation occurs, balancing that possible additional need against the additional costs of storage, and the potentially high costs of finding and retrieving them, that will be imposed by the added retention becomes necessary.

That's where risk management analysis comes into play. You can't just keep all your old records against the possibility that someone someday will initiate a lawsuit or investigation. As noted earlier, this type of records retention policy is both costly and either impractical or impossible; but it's also unnecessary. Some possible risks are so unlikely that tailoring a retention schedule to guard against them is unnecessary. In other cases, the cost of maintaining the records for the additional period is so excessive that it's not worth doing based on the likelihood of the event occurring and its probable magnitude. In all other cases, you have to do a balancing test. Your job is to perform the analysis that successfully performs this balancing act.

Any event that is likely to require the need to produce a record after the statutory and business retention requirements are met is subject to an increasingly small chance of occurrence over time. Consider, for example, a record potentially relevant to a slip-and-fall case. If someone is injured, there may be a very real possibility that they'll file a complaint or sue. However, most of the suits will get filed within a couple of years. A few people will wait longer, but the longer they have gone without suing, the less likely they are to sue in the future. Statistically speaking, you will have relatively many lawsuits in the first couple of years, less thereafter, and as time goes on, still fewer in each succeeding year. Eventually, the statute of limitation runs out, and suits thereafter are very unlikely. It's always possible that someone could devise a legal theory that would get around the statute of limitation, but this occurrence would be rare indeed. If this situation were graphed out, it would look something like the following, where the vertical axis is likelihood of suit, and the horizontal axis is the passage of time:

> Some possible risks are so unlikely that tailoring a retention schedule to guard against them is unnecessary. In other cases, the cost of maintaining the records for the additional period is so excessive that it's not worth doing based on the likelihood of the event occurring and its probable magnitude.

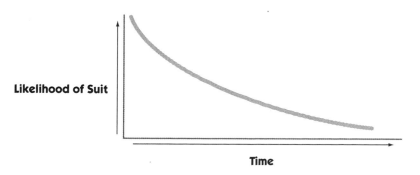

Likelihood of Suit

Time

Remember that, in most cases, this process plays out over a relatively short period of years, but the period could be much longer. In the most extreme cases, in situations where occupational disease related to chemical exposure is great, or where environmental contamination is involved, the possibility of a claim for latent injury showing up many years later may be very real, and along with it, the possibility of claims and legal actions. This possibility explains the sometimes very long legal retention periods for records of this sort, but it also plays heavily into the risk management component of retention scheduling.

Although statutes of limitation are often used in making risk analyses, they are by no means determinative. Statutes of limitation don't require any records to be kept. Their function is to set forth a period of liability within which an organization can be sued over one kind of dispute or another. This window of liability is only a *theoretical* one. In many cases, the actual period of risk may be much shorter than the nominal window of liability created by the statute of limitation. For example, finding statutes of limitation governing contract disputes that run as long as twenty or thirty years after termination of the contract, is not uncommon. Superficial analysis might therefore dictate keeping contract-related records for as long as thirty years after contract termination. As a practical matter, however, most contract disputes are raised and resolved long before this time. Regardless of what the statute of limitation provides, a dispute or lawsuit over a contract terminated thirty years earlier is an extremely rare event, and virtually unheard of for most kinds of contracts. Keeping contract-related records for the entire thirty years would in this case constitute serious overkill.

On the other hand, thirty years might not be enough in the case of the toxic exposure and environmental cases mentioned earlier. In cases where the injury is hidden, the statute is *tolled*, or suspended, until the injury is discovered, and only then begins to run. In the case of some environmental actions, there is no statute of limitation, and liability may accrue forever. In cases such as these, any finite period stated in a statute of limitation is largely irrelevant. You may be called upon to prove what you did or didn't do decades ago, regardless of the limitation period.

In order to make sound risk-management records retention decisions, it's necessary to have some understanding of the kinds of claims, lawsuits, investigations, and other such activities that your organization is subject to. This information includes not only the nature and frequency of the actions themselves, but also the kinds of records involved, the magnitude of the risk involved in monetary or other terms, and the time frames within which they occur. This knowledge permits you to perform the by-now familiar balancing act, wherein you try to make the choice that best balances the risks, costs, and

> Statutes of limitation don't require any records to be kept. Their function is to set forth a period of liability, within which you can be sued over one kind of dispute or another.

rewards of each factor in question. If you don't have this knowledge, there's a tendency to assign retention periods based upon imagined worst-case hypothesizing. The imagined risks are usually much worse, much more frequent, and go back much further in time than do real risks. As a result, retention periods are established that drastically overcompensate for the real risk that may be there.

Research, Trending and Analysis, Historical and Cultural Requirements, and Other Needs

An organization's management team may know that the organization is earning money today, but how does the current profit compare to five years ago? They know that they make pretty good widgets, but is the quality better than it was five years ago or worse? This information is important to know, but difficult to find out whether all records that would answer the question have been thrown out. Likewise, the organization and its work may have a history worth recording, or some other long-term purpose for records that is not strictly related to day-to-day activities. Thus, some records find a second life as research, trending and analysis resources, or historical, archival, and cultural records.

There's no general rule about what does and does not fall into any of these five categories; but there is a general rule about determining what should fall into them: ask the experts. There are important reasons for consulting an expert. Amateurs who are guessing (and amateurs are *always* guessing) usually guess wrong. Worse, they tend to drastically overestimate the long-term value of records, often resulting in historical or archival designations for vast quantities of day-to-day records that have no long-term historical value at all. This type of mistake is no trivial matter. Records designated as having long-term research or archival value generally wind up stored someplace more or less permanently, and if things are done right, it's a kind of storage and management that is considerably more expensive than the usual records-in-a-box-in-a-warehouse dead storage. Remember that you are building a research and historical repository; so, things have to be well-organized and accessible and stored in conditions conducive to long-term preservation. That's a costly proposition and thus should be reserved for records that are really worth all that trouble and money; the reality is that most records aren't. Regardless of what the purchasing manager thinks, future historians will *not* be interested in 2,000 boxes of administrative services contracts. Don't let him or her tell you otherwise.

So, if you are thinking of long-term retention of records for some non-business purpose, whether it is business-related trending and analysis or historical and archival preservation, it will be necessary to locate qualified personnel who have experience in these areas and work with them to determine what records are suitable for preservation and, as applicable, to determine a retention period for them. You will need to work with business research units, archivists, and historians. If you are thinking of an archival or historical records program and your organization doesn't have qualified archival or historical personnel, including yourself, you would be well advised to bring in such a person to consult on the project. Historical appraisal is not a job for amateurs.

Working with these personnel rather than just asking them for a list of records and retention periods is important. Archivists and historians may default to long-term preservation for lots of records just because of the nature of their business. For other records, saying "permanent" rather than thinking about a real retention period is easier, when in fact, records retained for trending and analysis or similar needs may have value for those purposes for only a few years. None of these personnel are necessarily sensitive to the cost or risk-management aspects of long-term retention; so, part of your job is to make sure that this consideration is included in the decision process.

Determining a Retention Period

After considering what factors go into a retention period, determining one is a straightforward process.

First, you begin with a business need. You can't, or at least shouldn't, get rid of a record before you're through using it. Active business use determines the minimum retention period for a records series. Next, determining any legal requirements gets a little trickier. As previously noted, there may be more than one legal requirement applicable to a record, and some of them may be vague or otherwise of dubious applicability. Therefore, you may have to make some judgment calls as to whether some legal requirement really applies. Once you've made a final decision on what does and does not apply, you line up your requirements and apply the longest of them to the series. What if no legal requirements apply to a records series? Simple. In that case, the result of this analysis is a zero. The business retention period isn't extended at all.

This analysis may provide you with some insight about potentially rearranging the structure of your retention schedule. You might, for example, have a big-bucket records series for accounting records; but after lining up and analyzing your requirements, you realize that ledgers and journals must be kept ten years, but other accounting records only three. This might be an opportunity to reduce the retention period for other accounting records by breaking up the series into smaller buckets. However, once you've got your buckets finalized and your requirements lined up, there's no fudging here. The longest period applicable to the bucket applies.

If you do otherwise, you are apparently breaking the law (at least if your analysis of the requirements is correct), and doing such is a very bad idea. At the beginning of this book, the topic of spoliation, or intentional destruction of evidence, was discussed. If an adversary in a lawsuit or other legal action thinks that you have violated a legal recordkeeping requirement, they will likely raise a spoliation claim against you. If they do, they're on solid legal footing and their prospects of prevailing on that claim are good. You can juggle your structure to get buckets with shorter retention periods and reduce those periods to bare minimums; but at the end of the day, if a requirement applies to a record, that's the end of the analysis—the retention period must be at least that long.

If you have records subject to maximum retention periods, you have to add those requirements into the mix. The maximum periods put a check on any thought you may have had of adding a couple of years to your retention periods as a fudge factor. If there's a maximum retention period in play, the fudge factor can only extend as long as the maximum period, unless you're willing to break out your schedule by jurisdiction to accommodate both your fudge factor and the maximum period. Hopefully, you won't have a situation where conflicting maximum and minimum periods from the same jurisdiction apply to the same records series. If this situation happens, your buckets are about to get smaller. You have to parse out your buckets until you get to a point where the information that is subject to the maximum period is in a different bucket from the information subject to the minimum period. Then, you can properly apply the two retention periods.

Next, you need to address the question of risk management, and things get trickier still. You now have a retention period based on business needs and legal requirements, and it's time to decide whether some risk management issue justifies keeping the records longer. Sometimes the analysis is straightforward; the retention requirement for your accounting records is three years, but the period within which you can be audited is the last six years. You could, if you chose, go into the tax audit without that last three years of records, but after sober reflection, and recognizing the fact that any deduction not supported by a record can be disallowed, you conclude that you would rather have the records. Thus, you choose a six-year retention period.

Other times, this decision is not so easy. Remember, once you have complied with legal requirements, there's no obligation to keep a record any longer. You can, if you like, simply go into an audit, investigation, lawsuit, or other situation without the record; and in theory, the other side is simply out of luck. On the other hand, some future issues are predictable, and experience may teach that being able to respond to inquiries and answer questions for some period of time is worthwhile. Your job is to balance that potential value against its cost. When you are doing so, you have to add in some complicating factors.

Regardless of bare legal formalities, you may at some point be judged on whether your retention decisions met a vaguely articulated standard of whether those decisions were "reasonable."

The first of these complications is the "reasonableness" factor. Regardless of bare legal formalities, you may at some point be judged on whether your retention decisions met a vaguely articulated standard of whether those decisions were "reasonable." What does reasonable mean? Hard to say, because the decision will be made by a particular judge or jury you haven't met yet. Bear in mind, however, that the question of reasonableness is likely to be raised by someone that is not very happy with the fact that your records aren't available to them. Some questions that are likely to come up might be like the following:

1. "Why did you extend the retention period for record X but not for record Y? What's in record Y that you don't want us to see?"

2. "Keeping all your records for ten years or longer would have been easy. Why didn't you do so?"

3. "The retention period for record X is ten years, but the retention period for record Y is only three years. Why the difference?"

4. "This retention schedule is just a sham to cover up your destruction of evidence, isn't it?"

5. "A retention period of one year for this record is pretty short, isn't it?"

Certainly more questions could be raised, but you get the idea. Someone doesn't like your retention schedule and would like to point out to a judge or jury that it, or something on it, is unreasonable. If they succeed, bingo! Spoliation. In order to avoid or counter this issue, your job is to make decisions on the retention schedule that can be justified as objectively reasonable. If you make decisions about extending (or not extending) retention periods, you make sure that you have solid answers to some of the questions that might arise: "Why this records series and not that one also?" "Why this many years and not that many years?," and so on. Likewise, if you're cutting retention periods to legal minimums, or applying short retention periods to records with no legal minimum, consider the challenges that could be made to the decision, and make sure that you have a sound response.

The second complicating factor that comes into play in risk management is attempting to forecast future events. One reason that organizations typically keep records beyond legal minimums is the perceived need to be able to respond to future legal issues. The question then is what to keep and how long to keep it. Knowing the answer to that question is based on the assumption that one can predict what those issues might be, how often they might occur, and how important they are.

Here, as in so many other places, there's no substitute for talking to the folks who know about the critical factors. In this case, risk managers, lawyers, workers' compensation specialists, and the other personnel in your organization who deal with complaints, grievances, lawsuits, investigations, and all the other issues that may involve your records. Many, probably most, risk management issues that affect your records have historical trends and patterns that can inform your decisions. Sound knowledge of those trends and patterns will permit sound decision-making and selection of prudent retention periods. Lack of that knowledge will lead to overkill, underkill, or some combination of both. None of these outcomes is good.

> Many, probably most, risk management issues that affect your records have historical trends and patterns that can inform your decisions.

Once you have a sound understanding of the pattern of events, you can devise retention periods that are responsive. As noted previously, it is a balancing act. Keeping everything forever is probably overkill, and not keeping anything beyond bare minimums is probably underkill. What's the best compromise?

That answer will vary by issue and by record type. As previously noted, the additional period of retention will impose quantifiable additional costs for storage, and possibly for partially quantifiable costs for search and retrieval over the additional life of the records. These costs must be balanced against the likelihood of future litigation (or investigation or whatever), the magnitude (or more crassly, the dollar value) of the litigation, and the period of time within which the risk of litigation exists. Also, you have to factor in the value of the records in resolving the underlying issue, and somehow come up with a result that is "reasonable." Your goal is to pick a point that accommodates most of the risk (and thereby maximizes the value of the invested cost), but doesn't go so far that you are spending large amounts of money on excessively low-value or low-probability risks.

At the end of your deliberations, you're going to select a retention period, and in almost all cases, it will be a finite period of years. That means that there is a point in time beyond which, if someone wants a record, it will not be there. If they don't like it, your response will be that what you have done is perfectly proper, and the fact that it's not available is just too bad for them. It's worthwhile to bear in mind the absence of records at some point in time as you are considering retention periods. To avoid not having records available is certainly not an excuse for making all your retention periods "permanent" or some such thing, but it is something you should keep in mind. Someday, you may have to tell someone that one or more requested records are no longer available.

After you have completed your risk management considerations, you will next attempt to determine whether any of your records merit long-term retention based upon research, archival, historical, or other similar considerations. If your organization is a government entity, the answer is outside the scope of this book. A number of statutes and retention schedules that not only provide exhaustive guidance on the matter are probably available, but also may even eliminate any discretion you might otherwise have had in the matter. For others, the watchword is economy. You can't tell your experts what records have long-term value, but you can hold their feet to the fire and make them justify their decisions. If there's a real reason that the records need to be retained for a hundred years, your experts will be able to tell you what it is. If you challenge the justification, they should be able to meet your challenge. Sometimes they can't, and five years or ten years turn out to be more than enough. As with the many other experts you will deal with in the course of your records retention project, there can be, and should be, some give-and-take and some debate. Conclusions that call for extraordinary costs or efforts should be subject to challenge and justification.

Trigger Events

A *trigger event* is something that must occur before a retention period begins to run. Trigger events are a complicating, and often vexing factor, in developing retention periods. In an ideal world, a retention period would be determined with certainty at the moment a record is created. For many records, the retention period runs from the moment of creation, and is thus known with certainty from the moment of creation. You may, as a matter of convenience, assign an arbitrary start date for the retention period at the end of the quarter or year, but that decision is in your control.

Trigger events are different. Some external event must occur before the retention period commences. Consider a contract, for example. The relevant statute of limitation might be six years; so, at first glance, selecting a retention period of six years for the contract might seem okay. The problem, of course, is that, although some contracts happen as an immediate, one-shot occurrence, such as the delivery of a load of gravel, many contracts are in effect for a period of time, often an extended period of time. You might, for example, enter into a contract for provision of electrical service to a factory that is in effect for decades, or perhaps indefinitely. In this case, disposition of the contract after six years would mean that you destroy the contract while it's still in effect—hardly a good idea. Your correct choice of actions is to choose a retention period that takes into account the life of the contract and allows you to accommodate issues that arise within some reasonable period after the contract is terminated. Your problem is that you don't know in advance when the contract will terminate; so, you can't reduce your retention period to a finite term of years.

You have to accommodate this uncertainty on your retention schedule by acknowledging that some event must occur before your retention period can commence running. That event could be one of many things. In the previous example, the termination of a contract is the trigger event. In the case of a personnel file, the trigger event may be the termination of the employee. In the case of records of construction of a nuclear reactor, it may be the life of the facility or building. In each case, the event, whatever it is, must be reflected on the retention schedule to alert users to check for its occurrence. As a practical matter, some mechanism to track events must be available so that users know whether they have occurred.

Trigger events are sometimes captured in legal requirements. For example, a common requirement for personnel files is that a former employee's file is retained for some period of years after termination. Many times, however, such requirements are not used in an organization. Equally common is finding requirements that state a period of years without a trigger event (the termination of employment), even though the requirement as literally stated makes no sense. In these and other cases, you will need to apply some common sense and ask a few questions such as the following:

- Does the record memorialize a one-time event, a series of events, or an ongoing relationship?
- If the events are ongoing, can users know in advance what the active period, or termination date, will be?
- Are these periods or dates consistent enough that they can be reduced to a finite period of time, or are they so variable that users can't anticipate them?

If you can't reduce that open period of time to a finite period, you're stuck with a trigger event. That's okay. In most cases, they're difficult to avoid entirely. On your retention schedule, you'll need to accommodate them somehow. That generally means concatenating them onto a retention period, for example in the case of a personnel file, EMP+6, where EMP is the period of employment and 6 years is the retention period. All that's needed then is for someone to track the occurrence of the trigger event.

Multiple Trigger Events

On occasion, multiple trigger events may apply to a single records series, which can be maddening. Implementation of a retention schedule is ideally a relatively rote process whereby a record is created, retained for some period of time, and then destroyed. When some set of legal requirements imposes different trigger events on the same record, it can be frustrating. When this happens, you must determine priorities. Does one control, or must they both occur? If only one trigger event must occur, which one?

Sometimes, you can't avoid accommodating them both (or worse, all three or four of them). Having multiple trigger events puts you into the position of creating a retention schedule that imposes a retention period of "First-occurring-of-this-or-that + X" or "Last-occurring-of-this-or-that + X" or "Upon-occurrence-of-both-this-and-that + X." Fortunately, multiple trigger events on the same records series are a relatively rare occurrence. It can, however, happen, and if the conflict arises because of legal requirements, as it sometimes does, it's simply something that must be lived with.

The Result

When all is said and done, you will have something that appears to be very simple: a retention formula consisting of a period of time that represents the retention period, sometimes preceded by a trigger event that must occur prior to the actual running of that time period. It is, in fact, not so simple at all. As previously discussed, the complications can be thick indeed.

The objective is to accommodate all relevant factors, while still keeping the retention period as short as is reasonably possible. The general trick is to avoid getting carried away by one thing or another. Every consideration has value, but in most cases, no one factor so overrides everything else that it skews the equation entirely in its own favor. Those occasions will, of course, arise from time to time, but your job is to recognize when an overriding factor is present, and when it is not. When you can make such decisions with confidence, you're on the way to becoming an expert in records retention.

Chapter 8

Laws and Legal Research—the Compliance Aspect of a Retention Schedule

It would be nice to think of a retention schedule as a purely administrative document that governs a kind of innocuous paper-shuffling activity, but it isn't. For virtually every organization, at least some aspect of legal compliance is associated with retention scheduling, and someone has to research some legal requirements and apply them to the schedule. So, now that you know something about your records and what your organization does with them, it's time to think about legal requirements and retention periods; and of course, that means that you have to start thinking about laws and legal research.

For smaller and simpler organizations, the legal compliance / retention requirement aspect of things may be relatively small and simple—a few tax and accounting requirements, and maybe a handful of wage-and-hour and other human resources requirements. For larger organizations however, this list can grow substantially. The number of potentially applicable tax laws multiplies with the complexity of the business, as does the number of wage-and-hour provisions. In addition, a wide variety of other requirements, often many hundreds or thousands, apply to various other aspects of the business. Depending on where your organization falls on this scale of complexity, your legal research project may be small and relatively simple, or it may be a substantial project. Regardless, you will need to be familiar with some concepts in order to tackle this end of the retention schedule.

Applicability of Law to Organizational Activities

The activities within an organization that are subject to records retention laws can be extremely broad. The short list includes, in addition to our standard examples of tax and human resources, requirements for workplace safety, environmental compliance, foreign trade, and other general areas, as well as detailed requirements related to many specific areas or endeavors such as pharmaceutical manufacture, energy production, nuclear activities, and many others. This list fails to do the complexity justice—within a broad heading, such as workplace safety or environmental compliance, any number of detailed subtopics may have their own detailed and very specific requirements. In a very heavily regulated environment where personnel safety or environmental compliance is a priority concern, for example mining, you might encounter laws applicable only to the inspection of cables on manlifts, or of ventilation blowers, sometimes each with its own specific legal requirements and required records and retention period. If your company is a mining company, this requirement is bad enough. If it's a conglomerate that runs the railroad that connects to the mine and the mill that processes the ore, as well as running other downstream activities, with their many other detailed and subject-specific requirements, you might find yourself having to manage a considerable number of very specific requirements.

Diversity of Sources of Laws

If all these many and detailed requirements came from one source, one might at least be able to read the local mining statute or consult with the local mining agency and come up with the list of records retention requirements. Unfortunately, this is almost never the case. Whatever jurisdiction one does business in, there's not only a mining agency or ministry, but also an environmental agency (maybe more than one, dealing with subsets of the environmental panoply, such as hazardous waste, or nuclear material), various wage-and-hour, workplace-safety and other human resources-related agencies, tax agencies or ministries, pharmaceutical regulation agencies, aircraft safety agencies, and so on. There may also be a great many statutes, such as taxation statutes, environmental statutes, and so on, that operate outside the jurisdiction of any particular agency. If you do business across jurisdictional boundaries, it gets worse—you have to account for these laws and agencies in each country within which you do business. In countries, such as the United States or Canada, not only is there federal law and a federal tax or workplace safety agency (among others), but also the same for every province or state as well, further multiplying the issue. The result is that the number of sources of legal requirements and actual requirements can be very substantial indeed. These federal and state and province requirements, combined with the detail of industry-specific regulation, is where the number of requirements that must be accounted for starts adding up, and sometimes turns into hundreds or thousands.

Statutes of Limitation and Other Nonrequirements

Other legal matters come into play as well. The most obvious of these legal issues are *statutes of limitation*—laws that set a period within which a lawsuit can be filed over an issue. Statutes of limitation, like records retention requirements, are topical. Most countries have, for example, statutes of limitation for contracts, various labor and employment matters, torts, and so on. Also common are specific statutes of limitation related to a number of very narrow legal topics or contained in a specific piece of legislation; and in some sort of catch-all statute of limitation for things not covered by a specific statute of limitation. In countries, such as the United States, statutes of limitation, like requirements, are also found at both state and federal levels.

Other legal concepts of interest may also wind up as citations on the records retention schedule. Possibilities include *audit periods* (periods within which an agency can audit your records), *audit cycles* (the agency is supposed to perform an audit every X years), and *abandoned property periods* (periods after which things such as the proceeds of uncashed checks escheat to the government).

Statutes of limitation, audit periods, and unclaimed property laws all operate on a retention schedule in a similar manner. Bear in mind that they do *not* impose any recordkeeping requirements, and it is perfectly proper in most cases to destroy records prior to the expiration of the applicable statute of limitation or audit period, as long as you are prepared to go into the lawsuit or audit without them. Statutes of limitation define the boundaries of a period of time in which there is a risk of some legal action that might involve certain records. For example, a statute of limitation for employment matters

> Statutes of limitation define the boundaries of a period of time in which there is a risk of some legal action that might involve certain records.

specifies how long after some incident that an employee may institute a legal action against you. This statute of limitation, in turn reveals information to you about how long records related to that matter may be useful. By knowing the terms of the statutes of limitation (maybe more than one) that may be applicable to some records series, you can begin to draw a boundary around the period of risk associated with the records. This boundary, in turn, may inform your records retention decisions.

Statutes of limitation can be broad, vague, or obsolete, and thereby problematic. These issues will require the use of some judgment on your part if you are contemplating using them on your records retention schedule. For example, you may encounter a statute of limitation for torts (basically, any legal wrong other than breach of contract), which is pretty broad. You could apply it to virtually every series on your retention schedule if you wanted to, particularly if you started imagining worst case scenarios. Virtually every record and data object in your organization would be subject to litigation exposure if you were to apply a tort statute of limitation. Likewise, you may find a statute of limitation governing disputes over "the payment of board and lodging to innkeepers, and to traders." Does this statute apply generally to contracts and commercial disputes? In each of these cases, you have to make a judgment call about whether to apply it and what effect it will have on retention periods.

Of course, as noted in the chapter on retention periods, the risk of legal actions is not static over time. It tends to diminish, particularly toward the end of very long periods. Some statutes of limitation run for as much as thirty years for such things as contracts, and retaining contract records for the entire thirty years will in most cases mean retaining them far beyond any real period of risk.

The Need for Research

A detailed discussion of how to conduct the necessary research in order to acquire all these laws and regulations is outside the scope of this book and is indeed its own book. There are a few things to bear in mind however.

- *Legislative collections are not going to be organized so that all your requirements are in a single place.* Instead, for example, one or more tax statutes containing retention requirements will be in one place, labor laws of various kinds in other places, statutes of limitation in still others, and industry-specific requirements in still others—all sprinkled throughout a large collection of books or a database containing thousands or tens of thousands of other laws that you don't care about.

- *The way that statutes and regulations are compiled into collections varies considerably.* The United States Code and many American state codes are broken down into topical titles, such as labor and environment, with topically related laws grouped together. Canada, on the other hand, compiles its acts alphabetically so that an act dealing with hazardous waste might be under "H," while an air pollution law might be under "A"—unless it's something like the Canada Business Corporations Act, in which case it's under "C" rather than the expected "B."

- *Some countries may not do much organizing at all.* They have simply a long list of uncodified acts, presidential or royal decrees, and other instruments that must be waded through.

Regulations are subject to the same vagaries, with the fortunate exception that at least the regulations from one agency will concern the same general topic. Consequently, you are inevitably condemned to a long and possibly painful session of legal research.

When approaching legal research, a key factor in reducing the pain is becoming familiar with how things are done and organized in the jurisdiction in question. Once you have learned the lay of the land within a particular jurisdiction, finding things is much easier, until you move on to the next jurisdiction and have to start over. In any jurisdiction, after you have gained some idea about how it organizes (a cynic might say "hide") its laws, you begin a laborious process of selecting promising laws, and reading through them to determine if there's a relevant records retention requirement, limitations period, or other provision of interest; and then capturing the relevant information for use on your retention schedule.

Finding Laws

So where do you find this stuff? The short answer is, "In a variety of places." The Internet is a good place to start. Countries, states, and provinces often have Web sites with legal compilations on them; and if not, sometimes particular agencies have compilations of the statutes they administer and perhaps their own regulations. The completeness of these compilations varies, as does the quality of any search engine that may be available on the site. Law libraries are another source; a really large one will have an exhaustive collection of at least the material for the country it's in; and a few of them have extensive foreign collections as well. If your needs are only for local law, the local courthouse may work just fine. Usually, a public law library containing that jurisdiction's statutes and perhaps some regulations as well can be found in the courthouse. There probably won't be much else, though. Regardless of which sources you use, be prepared to spend some time at it. You can narrow things down by developing good instincts for where to look and choosing good search terms; but inevitably, a lot of page-flipping, either real or virtual, and a lot of time goes into this process. The records retention provisions are likely to be buried within a much larger compilation of requirements in whatever statute or regulation they reside.

If you don't have the time to do the research yourself, other options may be helpful. A handful of commercial compilations of records retention laws are available. They can at least give you a start on what you need, and they may even be able to provide everything necessary. All these commercial sources have limits in terms of scope and comprehensiveness, however; so, if you use them, you may have to supplement them with some original work of your own or with material from other sources. Likewise, if you have the budget, you can obtain legal research from lawyers, such as outside counsel, or from a consultant who specializes in this sort of thing. In either case, it's a wise idea to vet the candidates and make sure that they have experience at records retention research. Not every lawyer or consultant is familiar with records retention schedules or records retention research. If they aren't, you may be paying them to learn how to do the research, at considerable expense and with dubious results.

Compiling and Analyzing Results

Eventually, you will end up with a collection of legal citations that are presumably applicable to your retention schedule. Then what? Your next step is to analyze and sort them. Like your records series, your citations are topical—each one is about some activity or operation, and some record associated with it. In order to apply the citations to the retention schedule, you have to know what topics your laws are about. When you have made this determination, you can match the topics of your laws to the topics on the retention schedule. Here, there's no shortcut for reading all your laws. In the course of collecting the citations, you had to read them all in at least cursory fashion in order to make a decision about possibly including them, but now you need to study them in much more detail. You must understand not only exactly what records each citation applies to, but also exactly what its retention or other requirements are.

This is also where you determine and compile trigger events, exceptions, and similar information that will affect retention, as well as other records management requirements not related to your retention schedule, such as media or location restrictions, and electronic signature requirements.

The Need to Interpret Requirements

As a general proposition, laws break out into fairly straightforward categories such as tax and accounting, workplace safety, and so on, at least on the big-picture level. On a more granular level, however, you will sometimes have to do some interpreting and some educated guessing as to what records the drafters of the law might have had in mind. The United States tax code is, for example, full of vague requirements to "keep such books and records as are necessary" to demonstrate compliance, with no other guidance as to exactly what books and records the framers might have had in mind. In other cases, the law in question is elderly or otherwise out of touch and is based on the assumption that you have paper ledgers and journals or some such thing. You have a decision to make about what data objects you may have that are legally sufficient counterparts to the specified but nonexistent items. In still other cases, the law specifies something fairly specific—say "a record of workplace injuries"—but it gives no clue as to the details of exactly what will satisfy the requirement. A one-line entry, like that on an OSHA 300 log? A detailed accident report? Medical records? In each of the above cases, you and your internal subject matter experts will have to use your informed judgment about what records must be kept to respond to each requirement.

On the other hand, as noted elsewhere, some requirements are quite narrow and specific, and they list the required data points in exhaustive detail. They may even require and deal with a single mandatory form. These detailed requirements can seem annoying because of the often lengthy provisions surrounding them and their own lengthy and detailed nature; thus requiring long and tedious reading to understand properly. They are, in reality, often the easiest to manage and to map to a retention schedule. They leave little room for doubt as to what is required or what is to be done with it. Subject matter specialists within that area of your organization are likely to be very familiar with what is required, as well as with any mandatory forms or other related matters.

Detailed requirements are also an excellent opportunity to cross-check your records listing or records series structure. If you have a list of legal requirements that you are sure apply to your organization, every record or data object referenced on them must be accounted for by your retention schedule. If one or more record or data object is not on the schedule, your retention schedule is incomplete. Perhaps your organization is not creating or maintaining some record required by law, but at the very least, it's something that you overlooked during data gathering and need to correct.

Privacy and Data Protection Laws

If you do business in Canada, Europe, in parts of Latin America, or in the Far East—and increasingly, in the United States—one thing you will have to consider carefully on your retention schedule is the issue of legally enforceable maximum retention periods. These retention periods are increasingly common as a tool for controlling the use and dissemination of personal information. A broad range of information is subject to requirements such as the European Data Privacy Directive and its national implementing legislation. This species of legislation prohibits keeping personal information longer than necessary and permits its use only for the originally intended purpose. Virtually all information about a person—whether an employee, customer, or someone else—is subject to this general rule in much of the world. If such a data privacy law is applicable to your organization, this requirement alone may require you to rethink retention periods, particularly if you are retaining personal information for downstream research and marketing purposes or other uses not part of the original data collection rationale. Fortunately, these broad rules don't call for a specific retention period. You have some leeway, as long as you comply with any reuse restrictions.

Additionally, specific requirements are associated with an increasingly wide spectrum of personal information. Medical information and some kinds of financial and other information are subject to a patchwork of specific, often quite short retention periods that require the information to be destroyed or purged within some specific time after collection. In some cases, the retention periods are only days or weeks, as compared with the periods of years that are the norm on retention schedules. Worse, these requirements sometimes apply only to a narrow bit of data that may be only a small part of a larger record that might otherwise have a much longer retention period. If you've gone big bucket, these requirements might shoot some holes in your buckets and force you to create some very narrow buckets to accommodate them. The issue might also have a real impact on how data is assembled into records, how those records are managed, and how the systems upon which the electronic ones reside are configured and managed. At this point, there's no uniformity as to what information is governed by these requirements. The list varies by jurisdiction, and it increases over time. International retention schedules are discussed in Chapter 10, but this situation may require you to consider whether you want a global retention schedule, one for theaters of operation, or one with exceptions for particular jurisdictions.

Excessively Long Retention Periods

At the other extreme, you will sometimes find some citations with very long requirements in them. Sometimes, they are topical and predictable, as with records that may document persistent environmental problems such as groundwater pollution. Sometimes, however, records that are subject to ordinary and reasonable retention periods in most places are subject to a very long retention period in one or a handful of jurisdictions. Thus, you may potentially retain all payroll records for fifty years because of a law that governs about one-half of one percent of your payroll records.

If you find yourself in this situation, you're once again faced with the big bucket-little bucket issue, along with the related issue of whether you need to break out individual countries or theaters of operation in order to wind up with a reasonable retention schedule. If the requirement is a narrow one, or in a single jurisdiction, you can perhaps manage by exception. Or, perhaps you can juggle your buckets on the retention schedule, legal index, or both, and isolate the offending requirements in a small and narrowly constructed set of buckets applicable to only a few records.

Here, fortunately, you have a bit of leeway. As long as you're not violating any privacy-related maximum retention periods, you can keep some records for longer periods to accommodate a longer requirement. The question is more often one of reasonableness and cost and of whether the electronic systems upon which the records are likely to reside can support the data through fifty years of growth and *migration*. If you find yourself stuck with longer retention periods than you would like, it's not a legal violation. Here, as in so many other places, the analysis and ultimate solution are a balancing act, where cost and manageability compete against necessity and requirements.

> As long as you're not violating any privacy-related maximum retention periods, you can keep some records for longer periods to accommodate a longer requirement.

Synthesizing Your Results

Organizing a list of legal citations for a retention schedule is partly an exercise in straightforward grouping and classification, and partly a process of informed judgment and art. On one hand, some provisions will speak directly to such things as personnel files, payroll records, and so on, and even call them out by name, permitting very easy organization of the citations and assignment of them to records series.

On the other hand, there will be vague requirements or broad statutes of limitation. Does a provision that calls for retention of "accounting records" apply to just the electronic database, or just to the paper records that form the basis of the entries in the database, or to both? And does that provision mean having to keep every scrap of paper with accounting numbers on it and every spreadsheet created, or just some? Does that thirty-year general statute of limitation really apply to all your records?

There's no hard answer in any of these cases. As noted for developing a retention schedule structure, your process for resolving these issues will be iterative. You group your citations and apply them, and see whether you can live with the results. If not, you try again, and see whether you can live with the results. If the citations are grouped correctly, but you're still coming up with retention periods that are problematic, you restructure the records series, and see if that helps. Along the way, you have to keep an eye out to make sure that your regrouping and reordering don't violate any legal requirements or create any patently silly outcomes. Eventually, you end up with the best compromise that you can achieve, which is what you have to live with. If it's any consolation, remember that those legal requirements weren't intended to make your life easier, or to permit you to destroy records at an early date. They are there to make sure that the records and the issues behind them stay around for a while. Given this purpose, if you achieve a reasonable compromise on retention periods, you've done as much as you can do.

> Exactly what you do with your citations after you have analyzed them depends on the structure and complexity of your schedule.

Organizing and Formatting Your Results

Most retention schedules will rely at least in part on statutory requirements, statutes of limitation, and other legal authorities for retention periods. There may in addition be other authorities, such as industry associations, that publish guidance that the organization treats as authority on retention periods as well. Now that you've gone to the trouble to find and analyze these authorities, you will undoubtedly want to retain your results for future reference. And if you've gone to the trouble to match these authorities to your retention schedule, what better place to make a formal record of the matching than on the schedule itself? Exactly what you do with your citations after you have analyzed them depends on the structure and complexity of your schedule. If the number of citations is not great, they can be mapped directly to the records series. If the number is large, you will need to aggregate them in some manner to keep track of things, and to avoid a cumbersome and confusing display. As you do the aggregating, you must somehow track any trigger events or other complications. The next sections address general formats for organizing and formatting search results.

Citation Numbering

In this scheme, you maintain a list of the legal citations found in your research and number them consecutively. The citations may be in some alphanumeric order, or perhaps just randomly listed. The list might look something like this:

1. 29 CFR 1910.220
2. 26 CFR 1.601.1
3. 40 CFR 60.111

and so on until you have

50. 47 CFR 490.47

These citations are then matched to records series by formatting the retention schedule as a tabular document, with the numbers attached to each records series collected in a cell at the right of the table, something like this:

Records Series	Citation List
Accounting	5, 6, 11, 24, 25, 31
Human Resources	1, 17, 22, 39, 41
Environmental Compliance	3, 45, 47, 49

This approach has the virtue of being reasonably simple, but it has some downsides that should be considered. First, if the number of citations is large, the box for each series can become quite crowded. For example, a retention schedule governing all the United States and all Canadian provinces would, if the research were done exhaustively, yield several hundred citations relating to payroll records, among several thousand other citations. Picking out hundreds of citations from a list this long and assigning them to records series

accurately is a challenging and error-prone proposition, as is accurately tracking their retention periods so as to ensure that when the task is complete, the
correct retention period has been assigned.

Then, the numbers for all these citations would be crammed into a box
at the right of the table, making them difficult to read, and posing a significant obstacle to any subsequent reviewer. To review the citation assignments,
a user must read each number, refer back to the citation list, and make a determination of correctness based upon whatever information is found on the list.
Like the person doing the initial assignment, they must, in the case of our
payroll citations, repeat this process several hundred times for this single
records series. This process imposes a serious practical limit on the amount of
review any such scheme is likely to undergo. This scheme is therefore only
suitable for situations where the number of citations is not large.

Direct Listing of Each Citation with Its Records Series

In this scheme, citations are listed in tabular format directly after their records
series. It might look something like this:

Records Series	Citations
Accounting	26 CFR 1.601
Human Resources	29 CFR 227.6

Retention schedules formatted in this manner often display a single citation
for each records series. As for payroll records, however, having just one citation is frequently not the case. In most cases, more than one and often many
citations will be listed for a single records series, and some citations will be
reused for more than one records series. The space and display issues of citation lists therefore come once again into play, and are perhaps even worse. A
small box on a table will handle a couple of dozen citation numbers. If, rather
than being represented by numbers, the citations are formatted on the schedule in the American style as "29 CFR 1910.220," space is used up much more
quickly. If they're formatted in the continental style and read like "Financial
Statements Act no. 448 of 2006," the problem is even more acute. Again, if
the organization is at all large or complex, there will be places on the schedule where the number of citations applicable to a particular series will be quite
large—dozens or hundreds. Further, you can't cram any meaningful information about a citation, such as its retention period, into such a format; so, some
sort of external citation list containing more detail about each will be
inevitable, and you're back to a citation list. Collectively these factors render

this method, like the citation list method, suitable only for smaller and less complex situations.

Citation Grouping

Perhaps the easiest and commonest method of aggregation is to create an index of laws similar to the retention schedule itself. Accounting and tax laws fall into one bucket; human resources, into another; and so on. By aggregating retention periods and trigger events, you can then derive a retention period for the entire topic, and apply this aggregated retention period to appropriate records series, confident that you've applied every applicable law. If you take this approach, you have the same big bucket-small bucket issue that you will face building the retention schedule. More on this topic, along with organizing your citations, is discussed later in this chapter. For now, just remember that using bigger buckets is simpler, but using small buckets lets you target retention requirements more precisely and apply shorter retention periods when requirements permit. Having built out a small-bucket index, you always have the option of nesting your buckets if it will simplify things enough to justify the likely increase in retention periods.

Using citation grouping is an attempt to avoid the problems of the other two methods by analyzing and grouping citations. For example, if your research turns up two laws related to payroll records and two records related to accounting and tax, you would separate them into two named groups something like this:

ACC-01
    26 CFR 1.601
    26 USC 601.225
HUM-01
    29 CFR 227.1
    29 CFR 440.6

On the retention schedule, these laws could be assigned to records series in a shorthand manner, like this:

Records Series	Citations
Accounting	ACC-01
Human Resources	HUM-01

One of the principal advantages of this approach when formatting a retention schedule is scalability: If continued research turns up two hundred more accounting citations and fifty more human resources citations, the formatting or display of the retentions schedule is not impacted. The supporting documentation containing citation detail may become very long indeed, and you may have a number of these groups of citations; but the link on the schedule between all those citations and the records series to which they relate has become very compact.

Mapping Legal Research to Records Series

Eventually, you will have two sets of data to work with—the records retention schedule and some compilation of legal citations and other authorities that you now need to map to the retention schedule. If you have done a good job of developing your records series, you should be able to skim the schedule and have a good idea of the topic that each records series covers. Likewise, if you have done a good job of organizing your citations, you should also be able to skim this list and get a good idea of what topics you have.

Mapping Individual Citations

If you haven't aggregated your citations into categories and are mapping them one at a time, the process is the same as it would otherwise be, there's just a lot more mapping to do, and a lot more tracking of retention periods and trigger events. One of the advantages of aggregating citations into categories is that it gets a lot of the work out of the way early. Being consistent is also tougher with one-at-a-time mapping if the list of citations is large—remembering what you did last Friday, several hundred citations back, can be a challenge. So, even if you're mapping citations one at a time, doing some organizing of them beforehand is probably worth the effort, just to simplify the process a bit, unless you're working with a very small number of citations.

The Correspondence Between Records Series and Legal Authorities

If you have aggregated your citations, you should make a pleasant discovery when you review the aggregation in conjunction with the retention schedule—many of your citation topics look suspiciously like the records series on your schedule, which should come as no surprise. After all, if your schedule is a functional one, your records series are topical, and your laws are topical as well—that's just how legal regulation is done.

This matching will make much of the mapping process a relatively straightforward proposition. You might, for example, have a records series entitled "Personnel Files." Likewise, your legal research will have turned up a series of citations that could also fall into a bucket called "Personnel Files." This correlation, when it occurs, makes for a nice, linear mapping, thus:

Retention Schedule	Legal Citations
Personnel Files	Personnel Files – Employment + 6 years

One-to-Many or Many-to-One?

Of course, variations are possible. You might, for example have gone somewhat big bucket on the retention schedule and wound up with Personnel Files; but you have smaller buckets on the legal citations, winding up with, for example, Employee Administrative Information, Performance Reviews and Job Actions, Benefits Administration, and so on. In other words, separate line items for various things that usually wind up in retention schedules. Why might this happen? Because the citations that govern these things frequently treat them separately. Thus, if you're breaking them out into the default topics as stated in the law, you wind up with a series of smaller buckets. In this case, if your retention schedule is bigger-bucket, rather than having a one-to-one relationship between the records series and citation groups, you have a one-to-many relationship, like this:

Retention Schedule	Legal Citations
Personnel Files	Employee Administrative Information – Employment + 3 Years Performance Reviews and Job Actions – 3 years Benefits Administration – Employment + 6 Years

Note that the overall retention period hasn't changed. In the first example, the same set of requirements is nested into a single bucket; so, the net result is still the same. It might also work the other way around. You might have smaller buckets on the schedule and bigger categories of laws. The relationship here would then be a many-to-one relationship looking something like this:

Retention Schedule	Legal Citations
Personnel Files Performance Reviews Benefits Administration	Personnel Files – Employment + 6 years

Of course, if you found yourself in any of these situations, you might look at the relationships and conclude that you could optimize both relationships and retention periods by same-sizing the buckets so that they look like this:

Retention Schedule	Legal Citations
Personnel Files	Employee Administrative Information – Employment + 3 Years
Performance Reviews	Performance Reviews and Job Actions – Employment + 3 years
Benefits Administration	Benefits Administration – Employment + 6 Years

Although not always possible or desirable, but when possible, this sort of rationalization can make for very clean relationships between records series and authorities and for smooth administration of retention periods. Likewise, you could find yourself in the same situation and opt to go big-bucket on both sides to achieve the same degree of linear mapping.

The Harder Cases

Other citations or groups of citations won't map as obviously. Statutes of limitation are a good example. They are often quite broad and could potentially cover many different records series on the schedule. Inevitably, you have to use sound judgment as to where they are applicable, particularly if you're permitting them to be a significant driver for retention periods. In order to map them accurately, you have to start asking what kinds of lawsuits could arise involving a given records series. The trick here is not to go overboard. Sure, you can imagine some situation where shipping and receiving records could be involved in an employment discrimination suit. However, in a case like this, where the relationship is pretty farfetched and the lawsuit pretty unlikely, you can dismiss that particular statute of limitation as authority for the retention of those records. If you don't, you'll find yourself applying every statute of limitation you have to every records series on the schedule, which accomplishes little.

Worse still are the occasional vague-to-useless requirements that turn up. Regulations for the U.S. Sarbanes-Oxley Act, for example, refer to the need to retain otherwise undefined "evidential objects." If the law in question is an important one for your organization and the retention period is substantial, careful analysis might be required before deciding exactly what evidential objects you're going to map to such a requirement.

Ironing Out Difficulties

If you find yourself having real difficulty mapping your citations to the retention schedule, something is probably wrong—either you have the citations broken out wrong, or you have records series that aren't as meaningful as they should be. In either event, it's time to do some re-organizing. Most actual requirements govern some specific process and records, albeit sometimes a very broad one; and most statutes of limitation govern some particular area of law, albeit again a broad one. They should, therefore, organize into reasonably clear categories dealing with various aspects of your organization. If you're having trouble breaking out citations into clear topical categories, you probably don't yet understand them well enough and need to do a bit more study and analysis of them, and then try again.

On the other side, you may find that some of your records series aren't really the clean, topical series you thought they were, but instead have wandered toward the hodgepodge side of things. This situation can make for tough mapping, because you are forced to map unrelated requirements to the same records series. In this case, your solution is simple: break up the troublesome series into cleaner, more topical categories. Have a look also at the titles given to your records series. It's easy to assign a title that sounds meaningful at the time, but isn't so meaningful two months later when you're trying to finish the schedule. Eventually, after a bit of juggling of citations and records series, you'll hit pay dirt. You will come up with concise and meaningful categories on both sides, and the mapping will come out cleanly.

Mapping may not be simple, however. If you have a simple organization and a simple schedule, with a few citations, or you've gone really big-bucket on both your retention schedule and citations, mapping may be pretty straightforward, with a couple of dozen fairly well-matched items on each side. However, if you have a large, complex retention schedule, you could easily have three hundred records series and dozens of categories of laws. It's highly unlikely that you will have one-to-one mapping on the entire schedule, and that means that there will be some complexity to the mapping, with a number of many-to-one and one-to-many relationships. Some care and patience is required. The mapping will drive retention periods, and careless mapping may result in retention periods that are too long or too short. Be prepared to spend some time at it, and to do some reworking if your mapping appears not to be working out as anticipated.

> The mapping will drive retention periods, and careless mapping may result in retention periods that are too long or too short.

Chapter 9

Electronic Repositories and Records Retention

Records retention when dealing with electronic repositories is not a conceptually different process than when dealing with paper or other media. For legal and compliance purposes, the contents of an electronic repository of any kind are the functional equivalents of their paper counterparts and are treated as such, including for purposes of retention and disposition. However, key differences exist between the records themselves and the ways in which they are managed. As a result, there are complications that may affect the way the retention schedule is structured, the retention periods on it, and the way it is implemented.

On one hand, electronic records may be formatted, stored, managed, and retrieved in a much more granular and accurate way than their paper counterparts. This difference is due to several factors:

1. Electronic records have various metadata attached to them that assist in search and retrieval;

2. Electronic records are text-, date-range, and otherwise searchable with automated tools;

3. Electronic records may be manageable on a data field or individual basis rather than on a box and records series basis as with paper; and

4. Databases and other repositories and records management software tools may permit detail handling, search and retrieval—and ultimately disposition—of large quantities of records with a relatively small input of time and effort.

Properly utilized, these attributes of electronic records allow for the possibility of extremely controlled retention and disposition of the records if the attributes are properly utilized. Proper utilization of those attributes will, however, likely require a considerable upfront effort. For records retention purposes, keyword searching and metadata can be handy. However, you will need to assume that it is the right metadata, that you know what metadata and keywords you are looking for, and that there is a way to utilize it to identify records for records retention purposes. Likewise, databases and software management tools can help manage records only if they have been configured to do so. Consequently, considerable planning and design effort must go into building or configuring the software repository or search tool so that the records in it are captured in a suitable data structure with the correct metadata and other search parameters.

That configuration can involve many things, including:

- Importing a retention schedule, file plan, or other data map;
- Determining suitable metadata fields;
- Defining capture methods for metadata (manual or automated);
- Defining classification methods for records (likewise, manual or automated); and
- Configuring the software to manage a retention schedule, including trigger events, legal holds, and other complications.

This list is, of course, the short one. The real situation may be much more complicated, and it may also involve a substantial employee training component to ensure that everything is being done correctly on an ongoing basis. Assuming that everything is done correctly and that the management software is state-of-the-art, records retention can be done on an extremely granular level, assuming that the retention schedule itself has the requisite level of granularity. Further, if everything has been captured properly with the correct metadata, execution of the retention schedule can be extremely accurate with relatively small effort and with little or no doubt that the proper items from the repository—all of them—have been properly purged at the correct time. In theory, this regime can be instituted beyond the boundaries of any individual repository to an entire organization, even a geographically distributed organization. Such is the power of well-organized and well-developed electronic records management resources.

Note, however, that this scenario is based on the assumption that everything has been done correctly. When things haven't been done correctly, the situation is not so rosy; and implementation of a retention schedule becomes difficult, problematic, or impossible.

> If everything has been captured properly with the correct metadata, execution of the retention schedule can be extremely accurate with relatively small effort and with little or no doubt that the proper items from the repository—all of them—have been properly purged at the correct time.

Limiting Granularity and Managing Technology

As previously noted, records management software may permit management and disposition of records on an extremely granular level. In theory, that's a good thing, and it may well be a good thing in practice too. However, here, as with so many other things, some prudence and care is required. You might, for example, find that your records management software is capable of supporting a ten-level-deep index, or maybe even a twenty-deep index. "Well" you might say, "I can certainly manage my records with incredible accuracy if I build a ten-deep index." And so you could, assuming that you can build a meaningful index with that many levels; and further assuming that your users will take the time to categorize things to ten levels. The first proposition is iffy unless you have some very complicated records. The second proposition is probably a non-starter. Unless you are working in some exceptionally controlled environment with some exceptionally disciplined people, you will never get other people to use that many levels with any consistency. You probably won't even be able to do it yourself.

You may likewise also find that your software is capable of working with other rules for such things as managing e-mail. Again, that's a good thing, but you need to temper your enthusiasm for the potentially limitless power of the software with the reality that in order to harness that power, you need to do good, sound design work up front, and the result has to be useful—and easy—for the personnel that will employ it. Otherwise, you are just wasting time.

The building of a coherent structure for your index and retention schedule are discussed elsewhere in this book. The rules don't change when dealing with electronic records, but the garbage-in-garbage-out rule very much applies here, which is worth emphasizing. Records management software in whatever form—*document management (DM)*, records management (RM), or *enterprise content management (ECM)*—doesn't actually manage anything. It helps *you* manage records by implementing rules that *you* create and that *you* configure into the software. No rules, no management; bad rules, bad management—it is as simple as that. Nor can it read your mind and divine your noble intentions and the clever structure and index that you have in mind. The only thing it will execute is what you design and put into the software. If you simply dump volumes of records into it with little thought, structure, or direction, you will have a big, messy, hard-to-deal-with pile of records residing in an expensive but useless piece of software.

> You need to temper your enthusiasm for the potentially limitless power of the software with the reality that in order to harness that power, you need to do good, sound design work up front, and the result has to be useful—and easy—for the personnel that will employ it.

If you are going to use RM software to implement a retention schedule, you had better be prepared to spend the time needed to do things right. In the first instance, that means building a sound schedule, but thereafter it means making sure that you have taken the time to understand the capabilities of your software, that the retention schedule is compatible with those capabilities, and that users know what is required of them and are willing to do it. Then, knowing these things, you have to take the time to configure the software in order to be able to do them. That means creating records series in the software, loading your retention schedules and retention rules, and making sure that they can be applied to the records series. It also means avoiding drop-down menus with two hundred items on them, records classification tools that require paging through multiple screens; and all the other things that discourage users from using a software tool properly.

Problems with Electronic Repositories

Notwithstanding your best efforts, it's likely you will be stuck with some situations involving sub-optimal electronic repositories. The things that might not be good from a records retention standpoint fall into a few broad categories, which are discussed next.

The Repository Management Software and the Records in It Do Not Support Good Records Retention Practice

E-mail is the classic example of this situation, but there are others. Several problems within the average e-mail repository include the following:

- Little or no data structure suitable for records retention within it, and no easy way to install one;
- The records themselves are not readily subject to rules of classification;
- No easy means of doing any classifying is available anyway; and
- No easy way exists to systematically purge records based on any classification that might be done.

This analysis could also apply to any number of other electronic repositories: sharedrives, Web sites, SharePoint portals, and so on. It also applies in a very big way to enterprise content systems—some aren't designed with records retention in mind at all, making the purging of anything at all problematic, much less the granular management and disposition discussed previously.

The Repository Has the Records Retention Capability— It Is Not Configured and Used Properly

Organizations often buy expensive records management, document management, or electronic content management software and install and use it without giving much thought to the matter of design, configuration, and proper usage, apparently on the theory that their records will self-organize after the software is in place. Reasons that such software is not used optimally include:

- An index or other data structure does not exist; or if there is one, it is not used;

- Personnel are permitted to use free-text indexing, resulting in large numbers of records categorized as "miscellaneous," "general," or the like;

- The software isn't managing retention rules; often, they are not even loaded into the software; and

- No thought has been given to the systematic capture and use of other metadata.

Usually, the problems inherent in this approach don't become apparent until a considerable number of records reside in the system and personnel begin having difficulties locating their own records. By then, there are simply too many records to go back and start over. So, you are stuck with a large mass of poorly organized and co-mingled records that you are now somehow supposed to apply your retention schedule to.

The Records Are Not Discrete Data Objects That Fall into Well-Defined Categories

E-mail can be one example of this problem. The e-mail may have two components—the message itself, and one or more attachments. The message itself could possibly be considered and classified as a memo or internal communication—unless of course, it is about two different things that fall on two different places on the retention schedule. The attachment—say a financial spreadsheet—could possibly be classified as a tax and accounting document. But what's the classification of the combination? If the text is about the spreadsheet, treating them as separate items might not be a very good idea, even if it were possible to do so, and no matter how good an idea it might sound like. If you did, and the items had different retention periods, you might well end up in a situation where a question arose about the memo/spreadsheet combination and you only had half of it still around. Other examples are common as well. Documents commonly contain hyperlinks to other documents, or to Web sites or portals, and understanding the document fully may require you to resort to the item on the other end of the hyperlink, which could be pretty much anything, anywhere. Consequently, establishing a retention period is difficult. Given that hyperlinks tend to get outdated quickly, it also makes maintaining any sort of long-term record of the entire thing for any period of time a real problem.

Financial databases and enterprise content systems are another variation of this problem. Everything is in there, but it is not in the form of the reports that you generate that appear to represent some sort of discrete records. Instead, it is all one big blob of interlinked stuff that may prove difficult, impossible, or prohibitively expensive to parse out into pieces for records retention purposes. The reports simply parse out bits of it and assemble them into what appear to be separate documents, when they're really not.

The Repository or Data Object Is Not Something Usually Considered a Record

Increasingly, legal requirements or risk management considerations dictate the maintenance of things like Web sites. Something like a Web site isn't a single record; it's a complex assemblage of what could be many dozens or hundreds of records of different types. Worse, the requirement to maintain the Web site is distinct from any requirement to maintain any individual records found on it. Rather, the requirement is to maintain a snapshot of the entire thing as it existed at some moment, which creates problems. A typical Web site is a dynamic system with constantly changing content, and collectively, it could be a very large item indeed. Retaining, not only all the content, but also all relationships between various pieces of content as they existed at a particular moment, will pose a formidable challenge. As far as the retention schedule goes, it's likely to wind up as its own records series.

Dealing with Your Problem Children

Whenever you are faced with one or another of these situations, you will find that your repository probably doesn't match up very well with your retention schedule. All your beautiful and carefully designed records series disappear into a swamp. In that case, it's back to the drawing board, either for the retention schedule, the repository, or both. You have to reconfigure the retention schedule to fit the repository, or the repository to match the retention schedule; otherwise, you are imposing rules that can't be followed, and that's not good. That means that unless your repository can somehow be reconfigured to a more organized and structured data set that more or less matches the retention schedule, you will be nesting your buckets until you get to buckets that match things that can be extracted from the repository. In the worst case, that means nesting up buckets until you have one that covers the entire repository.

Before you do any reconfiguring, you need to make a determination as to what is realistically possible with the repository, and what personnel can reasonably be expected to do on a regular basis. No point in reworking your retention schedule and coming up with a new version that isn't any more workable than the previous one. Blindly up-bucketing without some thought may give you buckets that are too large for other purposes. Thus, you have to look long and hard at how much detail can be imbedded in the system after the fact, or can be extracted from the system in its current state. The more detail you can somehow impose or extract, and use, the more detail you can leave in the schedule and the less nesting up you will have to do.

The question then is how much nesting are you going to have to do? If the repository is a reasonably well-bounded records set containing, for example, what amounts to the contents of personnel files, you may not be able to manage on a document-by-document basis (for example, deleting personnel reviews after three years). However, you can at least scoop them up into a broader category called "personnel files" and assign them a finite and reasonable retention period. If the contents are more of a mixed bag, the bucket gets bigger, and frequently its boundaries fuzzier. It also becomes less a rational description of a category of records and more a description of whatever hodgepodge is in it.

If you find that you are in this situation, it's worth doing some investigating. Such a grab-bag collection may well be all duplicates of records maintained elsewhere, in which case, you may not need to account for it on the retention schedule at all—it's more properly the subject of a duplicate records policy. If it's a really mixed grab-bag of material and you have no way of reasonably confirming that it's not duplicates or nonrecord material, and no reasonable way of sorting through it, you may have to be very conservative indeed, applying the biggest potentially applicable bucket—and longest applicable retention period—to the entire thing. That's painful, but your alternative is to set some arbitrary shorter period and hope that your decision doesn't come back to bite you during a legal action.

Other situations may also arise in which you are stuck with a big bag of legacy material, but you can perhaps manage the repository better going forward. In that case, you might wind up with two sets of buckets in the same repository—a big and conservative one for the legacy material, and smaller buckets on a going-forward basis. Eventually, the problem goes away—your legacy blob expires, and you can purge it. It may take a while; but remember, at times like this, very few records do not have finite lives. If you are willing to take the time to do a bit of analysis on the contents of the repository, you are almost certainly in a position to determine a worst-case retention period and thereafter out-last the problem.

Co-Mingling Big and Little Buckets

Any one of these problems may leave you with a situation where you have smaller buckets in many places because creating and managing them is possible. However, you have larger buckets elsewhere, including perhaps a few very large buckets indeed, because that's the best you can do. That's okay; but remember that you could be destroying things in the little buckets that may still be hiding in your big, blobby buckets. If you get a discovery demand, you will still have to search the big buckets and hand those things over. That obligation stays around as long as the blobby bucket does. When a discovery demand happens, responding to it will inevitably involve some cost and some pain—maybe a lot of cost and pain. Recognize up front that in this scenario, that pain and cost are a normal cost of doing business. Your alternative to the possible pain and cost of going through the repository later is to incur the cost and pain immediately and do it now.

As long as your buckets comply with any legal requirements, you shouldn't have any issues with larger buckets in some places based on technical limitations.

This big-buckets-and-little-buckets situation may also mean having to explain to someone why your records are still in the blobs but not in the little buckets. Isn't that some sort of spoliation? Well, no it isn't. You haven't done anything wrong at all in having big buckets and small buckets, nor can you be expected to do the impossible and somehow parse out a massive database. As long as your buckets comply with any legal requirements, you shouldn't have any issues with larger buckets in some places based on technical limitations. Just don't try to conceal the fact, and if called upon to explain, be prepared with your explanation. Resign yourself to the fact that someday you may be going through the blob very carefully for a lawsuit. This requirement, or the possibility of it, should be an incentive to minimize the blob problem as much as possible, and eliminate it as soon as possible. If you're going big-bucket, you want it to be a matter of choice and design and not of necessity, particularly if the necessity involves big, ugly, mixed-up buckets.

Old Backup Media

One place you are almost certain to find big, blobby repositories is wherever you store your backup tapes. There, you will typically find a large collection of full backups, partial backups, incremental backups, "archive" tapes, floppy disks, CDs, and various other miscellaneous backup media, almost always poorly identified, with a label that reads only "backup, 12/15/94" or some other such equally helpful tidbit. Further, a good many of the tapes and disks will be unreadable, either because of technological obsolescence or because they have physically degraded to the point that they're unreadable. What records series do you put all these things into? How long do you keep them?

Fortunately, the answer to this is usually pretty simple. If you're faced with this issue (or more likely, *when* you're faced with this issue) bear in mind the following things:

1. **For the tapes and disks that have degraded and can't be read, your work is probably done.** Restoring them is very iffy, regardless of what's done to them, a lot of the data will be lost, and very costly. Unless you have some critical, high value legal issue facing you, no one's going to spend that money, regardless of what data used to be on them.

2. **Backups are by definition duplicates of what is on your live system; so, no need to retain the duplicates if the live system retains the data for at least the correct period of time.** If you can confirm that your live system contains data for the period required by your retention schedule (and they almost certainly will), and there's no audit or legal hold requiring the maintenance of anything beyond that, then the backups should be treated as duplicates.

3. **People sometimes say that they are making an "archive tape"; but usually, they aren't.** That sounds pretty important, and it sounds like it should perhaps be retained for some long period of time. If they were really making an archive tape, a long retention would be true (subject, of course, to the reality of point 1 above), but usually, they are not making an archive tape—they're just making a backup tape and giving it a fifty-cent name. If it's really an archive tape, it should be a single-subject tape, containing say, the general ledger, and nothing else. Even then, what truly archival value does your general ledger have after you have completed your tax compliance obligations? Usually, not much at all. You should make sure that there is some very good reason for wanting to keep it for a long period of time, other than just the groundless fascination that people sometimes have with keeping a copy of things like the general ledger forever. You'll find only a few—if any—true archive objects in the pile.

4. **Because backups are for disaster recovery purposes, the only backup you need is the last one.** Anything else will be outdated and will not con-

tain your most recent work. That means that you don't need ten years of backup tapes. You need only the most recent handful.

So, knowing these things, what records series do backup tapes go into? Either they are treated as duplicates and not entered on the schedule at all, or they wind up in a category called "backup media" or some such thing. Either way, they get a short retention period—there is simply no need to retain 10 years' worth and many reasons not to. Remember that, if there's a legal action, you may be forced to go through them and look for things, and regardless of what you find, this will be expensive and painful. All those tapes cost money anyway, and re-using them after a short rotation cycle will save some money immediately. This is one instance where you can cut short the retention problem for big, blobby repositories rather easily, and you should take advantage of it.

In the unlikely event that you have real archive tapes with real, long-term value that extends beyond what is on the retention schedule, they will require special treatment outside of the schedule, since they are an exception to anything on it. Your job in this case is to remember that in the event of lawsuits or other legal actions, archival repositories must be searched just like any other repository, and plan accordingly. That reality may convince you and others that the repositories are not really so archival after all.

Chapter 10

International Retention Schedules

A few of the issues that you will face in creating an international retention schedule were mentioned in previous chapters. They are discussed in more detail in this chapter.

An international retention schedule isn't conceptually different than a single-country schedule. You still have categories of records in the form of records series, and you still have business needs, legal requirements, and risk management driving retention periods. Further, from a functional perspective, pretty much the same general categories of records are used everywhere as well, which shouldn't be surprising. Areas such as accounting, human resources, and various operational areas are basically the same no matter where you are. Of course, differences do occur—individual record titles will vary by country or region—and of course by language. They may be used somewhat differently as well. These variations usually map fairly well to your retention schedule, however. If you have built a sound structure for your retention schedule, with clean, well-defined, and truly functional records series, it can be adapted readily for use in different countries. Some things to keep in mind, however, are discussed next.

Variations in Your Own Organization

Your organization may not do the same basic operations in all countries. For example, if your company is purely a sales company, you may have virtually the same activities in every country in which you do business—marketing and sales,

> If you are contemplating the extension of a retention schedule into more than one country, one of your first tasks is to find out what your company actually does in each country.

human resources, accounting and payroll—and have the same functional record types everywhere. On the other hand, if your company is in the natural resources business, you might have a mine in one country, an oil refinery in another country, gasoline stations in several countries, and you also run a fleet of ships. All these business units will have unique records sets. A schedule crafted for any one of these countries will require some revision—maybe a lot of revision—before it is suitable for any other countries. Therefore, if you are contemplating the extension of a retention schedule into more than one country, one of your first tasks is to find out what your company actually does in each country. As noted in Chapter 3 on data gathering, finding this information may not be an easy task as, frequently, no central repository of this information exists; so, you may have to spend some time searching for the information.

Another task that you may find yourself doing is making the terminology generic. In the United States, for example, documentation for foreign workers takes the form of a particular document, called an "I-9 form." This form number is so universally understood that the term is generically used in the United States for files containing immigration documents and work permits. It is often used as the name for the corresponding records series. In other countries, however, there is no I-9. They have something else, and staff in other countries will have no idea what an I-9 is. Its generic replacement needs to be called "work permits," "immigration documentation," or some such name.

Another common area in which variations occur is where the schedule refers to specific laws such as the Sarbanes-Oxley Act. Strip out all these country-specific references or somehow note that they are applicable only in a particular jurisdiction. If you don't account for the differences, you will create a lot of confusion, spend a lot of time explaining things to foreign personnel, and then have to remove them anyway.

Legal Matters and Requirements

A second thing to keep in mind is that legal requirements, the level of regulation, and the philosophy of regulation vary considerably worldwide. Varying legal requirements will influence the development of a retention schedule usable in more than one country.

1. **Records retention requirements.** It is tempting to suppose that the legal requirements from your country will be adequate for other countries as well, but this isn't true. Records retention requirements vary considerably by country, and the differences are often extreme. A personnel file that might, for example, be kept only three years after termination of

employment in many places might well have to be retained for 50 or 75 years in some places. Requirements for other common records such as accounting records can similarly vary. From a records retention standpoint, these varying requirements can cause real problems, particularly given the trend to maintain these kinds of records in centralized, multi-country databases. Other requirements can pose problems as well.

2. **Paper vs. electronic legal systems.** Many legal systems are still paper-centric. Retention of electronic data or images of paper records may not suffice for legal compliance purposes, whatever value they may have for business efficiency. Even in countries that permit electronic records and images, they may be subject to digital signature or other requirements to be legally compliant. Likewise, there's sometimes a requirement that records be maintained within the physical boundaries of the country. In all these cases, the trend to maintain these records generically within a centralized database may pose problems, and it may require adjustment of the retention schedule to accommodate. In the worst case, you might find yourself maintaining the official copy of your accounting records on a shelf in-country to accommodate a legal requirement, while maintaining copies of your records electronically elsewhere for normal business use.

3. **Maximum retention periods.** An additional complication is the management of records to accommodate privacy laws. As previously noted, sometimes maximum retention periods apply, or at least a non-specific requirement to destroy a record after its original use is completed. In each of these cases, any retention periods based on requirements or business need for some minimum retention period must be re-evaluated in light of any applicable maximum retention periods. Privacy laws may also require an additional adjustment to the retention schedule because you may have to keep records of privacy law compliance, which means the potential for additional records series on the schedule to accommodate them.

4. **Miminum retention periods.** Retention period requirements could pose a real problem in cases where data subject to a minimum period is aggregated on a record with data subject to a maximum period, and the periods don't match. Not only is records retention a problem, but forms or databases might have to be redesigned to eliminate the conflict. This problem is further compounded if the data resides in a multicountry database also subject to other and potentially conflicting requirements.

Degree of Regulation

Some countries have very detailed regulatory regimes and as a result, detailed legal requirements for records management and retention. A large organization may find itself subject to dozens of statutory requirements, and often, statutory requirements are supplemented by regulations and other secondary authority that in some cases is longer and more complex than the statute it supports. The result can be hundreds of legal requirements applicable to the schedule. The United States, Canada, and Western Europe fall into this category.

On the other end of the spectrum are countries where records management and retention requirements are nearly absent, and many of the risk management issues, such as litigation, that are familiar to westerners are likewise not a serious issue. In such cases, even a large and complex organization may find itself subject to only a handful of requirements. Parts of Africa fall into this category. In between are countries in varying stages of building up their regulatory apparatus, and as a result, with varying degrees of regulation.

A further complication is the existence (and in fact, the expansion) of multinational federal entities. The United States is one of these entities. The fifty states are quasi-independent jurisdictions that can pass their own laws on many subjects. This independence creates two levels of regulation—federal and state. The Unites States is not the only such entity, however. Canada also has semiautonomous provinces that can and do pass laws with requirements that differ from those of the Canadian government. Other examples of multiple-jurisdiction entities are the European Union, Mercosur (an entity similar to the European Union composed of several South American countries), and Caricom (a similar organization composed of 15 countries in the Caribbean). Some entities, like the European Union, are very much on the track (at least from a regulatory standpoint) of having a fully federalist system with substantial regulation coming from the federal level. Other entities, such as Mercosur, have only partial federal regulation in such areas as customs and pharmaceutical manufacturing, but they are slowly expanding the currently limited scope of federal regulation. There are also single-purpose multinational entities whose member states subscribe to common regulations in such areas as pharmaceutical manufacturing.

You have to keep on your toes and periodically update your work to make sure that you are up-to-date with regulatory changes.

Each of these entities increases the total level of regulation within a country. Not only are there local laws to deal with, but also the laws of whatever federalist entity it is a part of. Since many of the member states are smaller countries that would not, under other circumstances, have had really extensive regulatory regimes in some areas, the net result can be a real expansion of regulation for entities within the country. In the case of the international retention schedule, that expansion means a lot more laws than you would otherwise have had to deal with.

Slowly but surely, the countries of the world are building regulatory structures in important areas like environmental quality and workplace safety, as well as the regulation of products like pharmaceuticals. Of course, every country is interested in the collection of taxes and duties. As a result, things change over time, sometimes quite rapidly. A country with virtually no workplace safety laws may, for example, enact a comprehensive workplace safety code with many records retention requirements virtually overnight. You have to keep on your toes and periodically update your work to make sure that you are up-to-date with regulatory changes.

Philosophy of Regulation

Countries take a variety of approaches to records and records retention. On one hand, countries, such as the United States, take a very hands-on approach to regulation and as a result have vast regulatory schemes. In an area, such as workplace health and safety, there may be hundreds of extremely detailed requirements for the maintenance of records of one sort or another. In some other countries, this plethora of records is reduced to a single omnibus document, the "Factory Register." In still other countries, it is reduced to a short and general law admonishing employers to maintain a safe and healthful workplace, with few or no records retention requirements. In each of these cases, the overarching goal is the same—a safe workplace. However, these countries have taken very different regulatory approaches that reflect the regulatory resources available for policing, the level of development of the country and its political and regulatory institutions, and the cultural and philosophical history of the country and its people.

> You will want to take the time necessary to get a feel for how things are done in each country into which your retention schedule will reach. Part of the trick is not just knowing what to do when you find something, but knowing what to look for and what to expect.

The privacy laws noted previously are another example of considerable philosophical differences that trickle down to the records retention level. Western Europe in particular, but Canada and other countries as well, have taken a very serious, very restrictive approach to the collection and retention of personal information. Countries, such as the United States, have much less restrictive laws governing use of personal information, and other countries have few or none.

These differences can result in the possibility of conflicts, such as those as noted for privacy laws, but they can create other issues as well. If you don't know that in a particular country all workplace safety records are maintained in the Factory Register, you may spend time looking elsewhere in vain. Likewise, you'll look for citations for other records that don't exist and needlessly puzzle over how to map citations to your retention schedules.

These examples are only a few of the more important examples of the differences you may find as you work through an international schedule and its legal authorities. The salient point is that you should expect to find differences and be prepared to accommodate them. You will want to take the time necessary to get a feel for how things are done in each country into which your retention schedule will reach. Part of the trick is not just knowing what to do when you find something, but knowing what to look for and what to expect. That knowledge only comes through familiarity with the subject matter.

Dealing with the Differences

If you are extending an existing retention schedule to multiple countries, it is best to think of it as a template that may require some alterations to fit properly everyplace it needs to. It may be a very good template, and need few alterations, but they are always a possibility. If you are just developing a retention schedule and have multiple countries in mind, you can probably build it to fit reasonably well from the beginning, particularly if you are familiar enough with the vagaries of international law and regulation to anticipate some of the issues. In both cases, though, you will want to be on the lookout for places where the kinds of variations discussed previously require some custom fitting to make everything work properly.

Retention Periods

The most obvious issue you will have to deal with is the question of whether you need a separate retention schedule for each country. The answer is, of course, maybe. There are other potential ways to organize it, though. You could have a single schedule applicable to all your countries, or you could break things out into a series of schedules by region, continent, or some other parameter.

This decision is really a version of the big-bucket-little bucket problem, except that now your buckets contain countries and not records. The problem is the same, though. In many cases, different countries will have different retention periods for the various records on your schedule. If you lump the countries together, that means that you have to lump their retention periods together and apply the longest one, just like you did when you were tinkering with big buckets on the schedule. If that longest period doesn't violate any privacy laws, and you can live with all the other downsides in the form of additional costs of storage, additional search and retrieval costs, additional periods of exposure during litigation, and so on, then the bucket of countries will work.

On the other hand, if you find that your bucket of countries is forcing excessive retention periods on you, or that the final retention period is being driven by a narrow subset of the records in the bucket, then you can break it up, just like you would any other bucket giving you the same problem.

The easiest way to spot the issue is to first create the schedule on a country-by-country basis, with rows for each records series and columns for each country. There's no downside to this process—you will have to capture requirements, business needs, and so on for every records series and every country anyway. You also need to line them up in a way that permits you to see whether some aggregating is possible. As you populate the retention schedule with numbers, you will begin to see how bad the news is and start making determinations as to how much up-bucketing you can do.

A single retention schedule is nice if you can manage it, but how much aggregating you can do depends upon the particular mix of countries you are dealing with and your organization's tolerance for longer-than-ideal retention periods. In a large group of countries, going single-schedule will almost inevitably lead to substantial increases in the retention periods for some countries. So, if you're going big-bucket on the records series and then big-bucket in aggregating countries, you may wind up with extremely long retention periods. How much aggregating you can do may also depend, as noted elsewhere, on the technical capabilities of whatever system your records reside on.

If your records are on a system that can't parse them out by country, and you have the wrong mix of countries, leaving you with one big bucket, you could again be stuck with some very long retention periods. There's also another flavor to this problem. As noted elsewhere—your system may not be able to parse records out by series. In the worst case, you have both problems—your records reside on a system that can't parse out records by either series or country, leaving you with one enormous records series. Here, you can only hope that the system is not the sole repository for your Russian personnel files with their 75-year retention period.

Lack of Regulation or Vague Regulation

Another problem you may face is that in many places where you would expect some sort of legal retention requirement, there is none, or effectively none. Worse, when you try to resolve the issue by consulting the relevant statute of limitations, it turns out to be thirty years, as is often the case worldwide. What do you do?

Your first step here is to make sure that there really isn't a requirement. Remember the Factory Register mentioned previously? Often, this document or something like it turns out to be the problem—there is a record and a recordkeeping requirement, but you are unaware of the local term and the local method of handling the issue. Once you have straightened out the disconnect, the mapping is fairly straightforward. In other cases, however, there

> In a large group of countries, going single-schedule will almost inevitably lead to substantial increases in the retention periods for some countries.

really isn't a requirement, and the record is one that is important enough to justify real effort to determine a suitable retention period.

Sometimes, looking at requirements from other countries provides a clue that there may be a regional, or even worldwide, consensus on a suitable retention period, or at least a range of periods, that you can then use as a basis for the retention period in your case. An obvious example of this worldwide consensus might be records of workplace exposure to hazardous chemicals or radiation. Most countries with a law on these topics have imposed retention periods in the range of several decades.

In other cases, however, you will need to make an informed judgment based upon what you know about the period of risk, likelihood of legal action, and other relevant matters. Here, knowledge of local conditions is extremely helpful in a number of ways. Sometimes, for example, that means knowing that litigation is not a real risk in the jurisdiction. In other cases, it may mean being aware that the information in question is subject to a reporting requirement rather than a retention and audit requirement. In this case, you still have to decide how long to keep copies of the report, but at least you are confident that the government is getting a copy of some information that you were pretty sure they would be wanting.

Privacy Issues

If your records series contain information subject to privacy laws and maximum retention periods and your list of countries includes countries where this is an issue, you will need to look carefully at both records series and retention periods. Conflicts are a real possibility, particularly if you are contemplating aggregating more than one country into a single schedule or you are going big bucket on your series.

If you have a record that is subject to maximum retention periods in several countries, the shortest period is the one that counts, not the longest.

A record subject to a maximum retention requirement *can't* be part of a records series with a longer retention period. It must be broken out into a separate records series for at least that country, or your series must somehow be reorganized so that the problem is resolved. If you leave it in the same records series, you are breaking the law, and that's a bad idea. Countries that have enacted personal data privacy laws take them seriously. Likewise, if you have a record that is subject to maximum retention periods in several countries, the *shortest* period is the one that counts, not the longest. As with situations where you are aggregating normal retention periods, the most restrictive requirement must be complied with. Once again, conflicting or unreasonable results may require you to dis-aggregate your countries and list them singly or in some other combination.

If the information subject to the privacy law is part of a larger record that must have a longer period, or is in a database or other repository that can't be managed on a level granular enough to permit you to comply with the maximum retention period, you have a problem that may require process or systems re-engineering to resolve.

Working Through It

As you can see, there are a number of situations where you will have to work through some thorny issues carefully. The more countries that you are dealing with, the more of this adjusting you will have to do. The trick here is to keep sight of the places where you have some leeway to make adjustments, such as lengthening a retention period, adjusting a bucket size, or whatever, and the places where some requirement is non-negotiable, and you have to rearrange things around it. As with most things on the schedule, at the end you will have an acceptable series of compromises that are less than perfect for many things, but optimal when legal requirements or other considerations demand it.

Chapter 11

Litigation and Other Legal Matters

A reality of life is that organizations of all kinds find themselves involved in lawsuits, audits, investigations, and other legal proceedings. One reason that governments require organizations to keep records is to facilitate that process. The records are available in order to assist the authorities in finding the facts and resolving the issues that present themselves.

Because records wind up in court, it should come as no surprise that records retention schedules and their implementation are also often involved in legal proceedings. That's one of the reasons you have a records retention schedule—it assists you in resolving questions about what records you do and don't have, and why. Records retention is more an issue in the United States than in many other places, but any place that you maintain a business presence and records may offer the same issue. Although possibly fewer in number in another country, legal actions involving your organization are always a possibility.

A retention schedule can act as many things—an index, a data structure, a policy, a procedure—but there are a few things it is not, and they are worth keeping in mind.

A Records Retention Schedule Is Not a Privileged Document

If you are involved in a legal proceeding of any kind and the records retention schedule becomes relevant to the proceeding, your adversary has the right to demand and obtain a copy of the schedule and any supporting or relevant docu-

> You should proceed on the assumption that, in the event of a legal matter involving it, the retention schedule and its supporting documentation are an open book that is available to any interested party.

mentation that surrounds it, including records of how you have implemented the schedule. Some things associated with the retention schedule *are* privileged. If, for example, in-house or external counsel gave advice concerning the schedule, this information may be privileged, as other things may be as well. You should always consult with legal counsel for a determination of what is privileged and what is not. As a general proposition, however, you should proceed on the assumption that, in the event of a legal matter involving it, the retention schedule and its supporting documentation are an open book that is available to any interested party.

Potential legal problems should not be a cause for concern. If you have built your schedule correctly, the retention outcomes that it drives should be clear and defensible outcomes, and you should be able to respond to any questions with answers that support them. Likewise, if you have implemented the schedule properly, the actions taken should be legal and defensible, and you should have no difficulty in responding to any questions about your implementation.

The retention schedule should, however, point to the value of having documentation that provides clear and unambiguous answers to potential questions. It also points to the value of having a schedule that itself provides clear and unambiguous direction to the personnel that implement it. The clearer the direction, the more accurately your staff will be able to carry it out, and the fewer concerns and issues to resolve later. If an adverse party in a legal proceeding becomes interested in your retention schedule, you can be sure that they will have a lot of questions. The better the schedule and its implementation program, the sooner many of those questions and issues will be resolved, and the less traction the remaining questions will have thereafter.

A Retention Schedule Does Not Eliminate Any Litigation-Related Duties

Retention schedules apply in the absence of litigation or other legal matters. Once a legal matter has commenced, the rules change completely, and clearly understanding those rules is very important. Once again, there is no substitute for close consultation with legal counsel, and obeying any instructions that they may give you.

Destruction of Records Related to the Legal Matter Must Cease

Regardless of the retention period indicated on your records retention schedule, if a record is relevant to a current or imminent legal proceeding, you cannot alter, destroy, or otherwise dispose of it. How do you know whether a legal proceeding is current or imminent? How do you know whether a record is relevant to one? In both cases, you should not consider yourself either empowered or qualified to make the call. Instead, you should work closely with legal counsel. They will make a determination as to whether legal proceedings are imminent or active, and they can provide you with information about the kind of records that must be preserved. They should issue a preservation order describing the kinds and dates of information that must be preserved.

Specifying the preservation of some general category of records such as "accounting records" or "e-mail" is generally not enough for counsel to do. Legal actions are about some specific matter and involve some specific timeframe. Therefore, your legal counsel should be specifying accounting records related to such-and-such transaction from such-and-such time period; or e-mail from such-and-such party on such-and-such topic. Reasons for such detail about which records should be preserved include:

1. **The scale of the records system may determine compliance with a preservation order.** A general requirement to preserve something like "accounting records" may well prove impossible to comply with. In a large organization with dynamic electronic accounting systems, preserving a snapshot of the system as of some moment may not be possible due to the scale of the system and the amount of data in it. Saving an image of the system state on backup media may likewise be impossible due to the number of tapes or disks required and the effective impossibility of creating an environment where the data can be restored. Even with paper records, a preservation order involving tens of thousands of boxes and unknown quantities of records in numerous locations may be effectively impossible to impose and enforce.

2. **Cost of compliance may be too high.** Even if you can comply with the preservation requirement, the cost of doing so will be extraordinarily high, and needlessly so. If, as is likely, the records needed are only a small percentage of the accounting or e-mail system's contents, most of the cost of search and preservation will be wasted. If, as in previous examples, the amount is terabytes of electronic data or millions of pages of paper documents, those costs can be very substantial indeed. In smaller organizations, the absolute numbers may be smaller, but so are the organizations and the available resources. Therefore, proportionally, the unnecessary cost to the organization is about the same.

3. **The most relevant material may be lost.** Because the legal matter is about a particular matter and a particular timeframe, the really relevant material is likely to get lost like a needle in a haystack, defeating the whole purpose of the preservation order. It is, to say the least, counterproductive to spend huge sums of money trying to preserve records for a

It is, to say the least, counterproductive to spend huge sums of money trying to preserve records for a legal action only to be unable to find the ones you need in the mass of irrelevant material.

legal action only to be unable to find the ones you need in the mass of irrelevant material.

4. **A narrow scope preservation order may save valuable time.** If you get a vague or generally worded preservation order, or have any other question regarding if and what records may need preservation for a legal matter, seek and obtain enough clarification to ensure that first, you are absolutely clear as to what records must be preserved; and second, that the demands being made of you and your program are feasible and not unnecessarily burdensome. If really burdensome demands are being made, again, consult with counsel—they may be able to narrow the scope of the preservation order, and if not, will at least be aware that they have made some problematic demands. In the absence of such knowledge, you might find that they have committed you to a production and delivery schedule that is unrealistic or will have you working weekends for two months.

Ideally, this communication and cooperation with counsel should begin prior to the initiation of any legal matters requiring records and records retention. You should have a procedure and process in place that sets forth the duties of each party, and the necessary workflows to accomplish the needed tasks. If one is not in place, now is a good time to develop one.

Records Related to the Legal Matter Must Be Segregated and Preserved

The last thing that you want to have happen is to identify a record as being relevant to a pending legal matter, and then have someone throw it away because they were unaware of the matter or the relevance of it. If this happens and an adverse party becomes aware of the missing record, they will be very unhappy and raise claims about spoliation, destruction of evidence, and other such things, and you will probably spend a lot of time in depositions with lawyers, stenographers, and videographers, and maybe in a courtroom as well, explaining what happened. If you are like most people, you find the prospect of this scenario disagreeable; so, you probably want to avoid it. The way to avoid it is to make sure that once records are identified as relevant to a matter, they are preserved and protected.

How this is accomplished will vary. In some cases, copies can be made, preserved, and used in the legal matter. In other cases, the original records must be physically segregated in some matter. In still others, the system where the records reside may need some additional controls and protection to prevent alteration or deletion. This again is an area where you should work closely with counsel. You can tell them what is possible and reasonable, but ultimately, they are responsible for making the call on whether to preserve, when to preserve, what to pre-

> The last thing that you want to have happen is to identify a record as being relevant to a pending legal matter, and then have someone throw it away because they were unaware of the matter or the relevance of it.

serve, and how to preserve it. Your job then is to execute the requirement as effectively as possible and to inform them of issues and problems if they arise.

The Role of the Retention Schedule

If your retention schedule has been well-crafted and well-implemented, it can be a substantial help during the process of identifying and preserving records for a preservation hold. The retention schedule plays four roles in an organization.

1. **The retention schedule tells you what you have and don't have.** That's a very good thing, and can be quite a timesaver. If the other side asks for six years' worth of records, and you have only five years' worth, you should know that up front, rather than spending days or weeks looking for that nonexistent sixth year's worth of records.

2. **Your schedule functions as an index in the absence of, or in conjunction with, other indices.** That means that you can easily perform topical searches of say, personnel files or hazardous waste records. This capability substantially shortcuts the need to laboriously page-flip your way through stacks of paper, or screen-flip your way through masses of electronic records.

3. **The schedule helps you explain absent records.** When the other side complains about the absence of that sixth year's worth of records, you should be able to demonstrate that their absence is entirely legitimate and avoid sanctions or other problems.

4. **A well-implemented schedule will have no major gaps or inconsistencies.** If the schedule indicates that a records set should still *be* available, it should be available, and any records series that should not be available should *not* be available. That significantly reduces the chance that someone will raise a spoliation claim, or that if they do raise it, that they will prevail.

You should not, however, consider the retention schedule as being the final, detail-level tool for identifying records for a preservation order. Remember, by its nature, a records series is a fairly general aggregation of individual record types, and the bigger your buckets, the more general the aggregation. Therefore, although the retention schedule may get you close to the records you need, it may not, and probably will not, get you all the way there. Within the records series, you are still dealing with subsets, and within those subsets, individual documents concerning particular people or transactions. If you have good document-level metadata, such as dates, e-mail addresses, and so on, they may give you further support. However, in many cases, the final, detail-level tool for making the determination concerning the absence of requested records will be someone's eyes.

Retention of the Retention Schedule

The records retention schedule is a record—a kind of combination policy, procedure, and work instruction. As noted previously, questions may well come up about it. Should you therefore include it on your retention schedule? For once, the answer is an unambivalent "yes." You could include it in a series with other policies and procedures, or you could give it a line item of its own. There are no doubt other possibilities as well. How you include the retention schedule on your retention schedule depends upon how your schedule is structured. Here are a couple of things to remember about scheduling the retention schedule:

1. **Legal questions arising from legal matters will more likely be about what happened several years ago.** They won't be about retention decisions you made last week. In the interim, you will likely have revised the retention schedule, perhaps more than once. Therefore, you will want to establish a retention period that goes back at least several years and accounts for any superseded versions of the schedule that cover that period of years.

2. **The retention schedule doesn't live in a vacuum—various other documents support it and document its implementation.** You might, for example, have some implementing procedures or work instructions. You might also decide to create forms, such as destruction certificates, to document the destruction of records pursuant to the schedule. If so, you will want to establish retention periods for these items as well, and their retention periods should match the retention period for your retention schedule. That way, you will have a complete record of what you have done for some reasonable and fairly long period of time. As with the other things discussed in this chapter, this detail will go a long way toward avoiding or minimizing many records management issues that might otherwise arise. A sample destruction authorization form is included in Appendix E, and a sample certificate of destruction is in Appendix F.

> The value of a retention schedule during a legal action is directly proportional to the quality of the schedule and its implementation.

The Value of Having Done Things Well

At this point, you likely have begun to see that the value of a retention schedule during a legal action is directly proportional to the quality of the schedule and its implementation. A poorly drafted schedule can result in any of a number of serious problems:

- Poor or absent legal research can lead to incorrect and possibly illegal retention periods;
- Badly drafted records series can lead to misclassification of records;
- Badly drafted records series can lead to confusion about whether a record has been destroyed;
- Badly drafted records series can make locating relevant records difficult; and
- Failure to document retention activities may lead to questions as to whether they occurred.

This list is by no means exhaustive. Any of these or other shortcomings, if they occur, can form the basis of issues that cause problems during legal actions and are counterproductive to the goals of any records retention program. The point here is that if you're going to develop a retention schedule, make the effort to do a good job, and make sure that it is implemented effectively. Only then will it be of value to you.

Chapter 12

Maintenance and Beyond

Once you have completed the building of a retention schedule, you can breathe a sigh of relief and enjoy the feeling of a task well done. But then what? Are you done with it?

The Need for Maintenance

Of course not. It's like building a house. Once the structure is built, you have at most a short respite—maybe none at all—before you enter into the maintenance phase. Light bulbs will burn out, faucets will need repair, woodwork will need painting, gutters will need cleaning, and so on. A retention schedule will likewise need some ongoing maintenance. Several important reasons for maintaining the schedule properly include:

- *You learn more about your organization.* The retention schedule you just completed is version 1.0.0. Unless your organization is very small and simple, it's unlikely that you've managed to learn everything necessary to make v. 1.0.0 an absolutely complete and optimal schedule. That's okay, but you need to bear that in mind, and as additional information comes to your attention, you should be prepared to make use of that additional information to further refine your schedule.

- *Your organization may change.* Large organizations get into and out of various lines of business pretty regularly. Your retention schedule needs to expand or contract to accommodate these changes, and as a result, records series may come and go as different business activities and their associated records become a part of the picture or cease to do so.

If your organization began small, it may grow. Industrial giant Hewlett Packard was once (not that long ago) a two-man shop operating out of a residential garage. Many other organizations, including such giants as Microsoft, have started very small and ended up very large.

When growth happens, the organization's records and records systems become more complex, the organization spreads to new jurisdictions, its legal and regulatory environment becomes more complex, and it expands its scope of activities. Each of these changes warrants a review of the retention schedule to make sure that it's still accurate and complete and does its intended job.

- *Records come and go.* Even in a relatively static organization, many of the specific records in use change over time as the organization redesigns its forms, changes its processes, or regulatory agencies issue new or additional forms. Over time, that change will accumulate to the point where records series need redesign or redefinition, or the need arises to add or delete series from the schedule. If your organization is moving into and out of lines of business, or acquiring or divesting subsidiaries, this process will be very much accelerated, and the degree of change very much greater.

- *Your records retention philosophy changes.* This could encompass many things: You went big bucket and now decide that little buckets suit your needs better; you went small bucket, and now want to go big bucket; you've become more risk averse and want longer retention periods; you've become less risk averse and want shorter retention periods; you've acquired some enterprise content management system and the retention schedule must be altered to accommodate it; maybe you've just reviewed the schedule and decided that you could do some things better. All these things warrant review of the schedule.

- *The law and the legal environment change.* Any time you start doing business in a new jurisdiction, or enter into a new line of business, laws and the legal environment will be an issue. Even in the absence of these things, however, new laws are enacted or old ones revised on a regular basis, and these changes may affect the retention periods on your schedule, or require you to accommodate additional records now required by law. Thus, regardless of whether your organization is evolving or not, you should be prepared to periodically review the legal basis for your retention schedule and satisfy yourself that your original conclusions are still valid and that you're still comfortable with them.

> Regardless of whether your organization is evolving or not, you should be prepared to periodically review the legal basis for your retention schedule and satisfy yourself that your original conclusions are still valid and that you're still comfortable with them.

The Maintenance Process

As a general proposition, the maintenance process has two monitoring tracks: first, you somehow need to periodically update your knowledge of your organization's internal changes—lines of business, records in use, geographic expansion or contraction, and so on. Some of this can be achieved by simply being an informed student about the activities of the organization, but you'll probably have to supplement it with additional data gathering. Thus, if you've designed survey or interview forms for your initial data gathering, they will likely find new life as the basis of forms used for periodic update activities.

The second process is the monitoring of external events such as changes to law. To some extent, this monitoring can again be accomplished by being an attentive student of legal and commercial affairs, but at some point you will have to dig deeper. Many relevant changes to records laws are buried within obscure and complex regulations that don't make the headlines. Even if you suspect that there may be changes to relevant law, you'll have to go dig them out of a law library or legal database.

Compiling Your Results and Adjusting Your Schedule

You will probably compile a list of action items throughout the course of the year. For a few reasons, it is unavoidable. Issues raised by your user community will trickle in over the course of the year as the users use the schedule and run into questions and issues. If you do an update survey, results will trickle in over time; if you do interviews, they will occur over a period of time; and other miscellaneous information will come to your attention here and there. Likewise, changes to law and the legal climate will occur periodically throughout the year and will come to your attention periodically, prior to any formal research that you conduct. Any new research you conduct will also take some period of time.

You could, of course, make adjustments to your schedule on an ongoing basis throughout the year and issue a series of revisions. As a practical matter, however, this is likely to be impractical for you and confusing for your user community. Making all those changes and getting all those revisions approved rapidly will prove difficult, and users will soon be annoyed by being bombarded with a constant stream of revised retention schedules. They will also be uncertain about the applicability of the various versions (does the March revision apply to a record created in February?), and that means that you will be bombarded with questions.

A better approach is to save up all issues and potential changes and make your revisions on a regular cycle of perhaps a year. There will still be questions, of course, but you'll only have to field them once a year. Once people are

> A better approach is to save up all issues and potential changes and make your revisions on a regular cycle of perhaps a year.

accustomed to the revision cycle, the volume of questions will diminish. Fortunately, most changes to a retention schedule aren't so time-critical that they can't wait for the normal revision cycle, and in the event such a change is required, it can always be done as a one-off exception to the normal cycle.

As far as analyzing your new data and making changes, the process is much like the one that you used to draft the schedule in the first place. New record types or new lines of business warrant an analysis to determine whether new records series are warranted. Either they map seamlessly into existing records series, or they don't. If not, either you adjust the series or add new ones, bearing in mind all previously discussed information about creating clean, well-defined, and well-bounded records series. The data that you have compiled should permit this. If it doesn't, you will need to obtain additional information, just like you did when you first drafted the schedule. When your new or revised records series are complete, you map your legal research to them, and if necessary, perform some additional research. New or revised laws are mapped to the appropriate records series, and retention periods are analyzed in light of them.

If you did a good job in first building your schedule, you will find that your schedule handles these changes with ease. You will have to add a series here, change a retention period there, and if things have changed a lot, you may have to add or change quite a few individual items; but you shouldn't have to engage in wholesale dismantling and rebuilding of the schedule in the absence of some extraordinary change in circumstances. Your basic structure should hold up well. You'll also find that the skills you acquired in your initial data gathering will serve you well here. The data gathering for a revision cycle will be relatively small and well-contained compared with the really large effort required for the initial building of the schedule, and by now you're a lot better at it, so you're likely to find that things go much smoother than they did the first time around. After the first couple of revision cycles, you'll also have caught many of the inevitable omissions and errors from v.1.0.0, and the revision process will become smoother and easier.

Am I Done Yet?

Nope. Although the scope of revision to your schedule will decrease over time, it will be a fixture in your life as long as you are a records manager. Beyond that, now that you have a retention schedule, you need to start thinking about implementing it. That means developing processes for identifying records eligible for destruction, retrieving them, destroying them, document-ing the destruction, and all the other things that need to be a part of the entire process; and of course, all this must be documented in written policies and procedures. Welcome, therefore, to the business of writing good, sound records management policies and procedures. For now, congratulate yourself! If you have gotten this far, you have completed a very large and important project and learned a lot about your organization and about records manage-ment in the process. For that, you can be proud.

Sample Records
Retention Schedules

Acme Corporation Records Retention Schedule

Abbreviations: ACT = While Active; EMP = Termination of Employment

	Record Description	Official Custodian	Business Retention	Legal Retention	Total Retention	Legal Reference
ACCOUNTING						
Accounts Payable	Records of amounts owed and paid to outside parties such as vendors and contractors.	Accounting Dept.	5	7	ACT + 7	AC.10.
Accounts Receivable	Records of amounts owed by outside parties such as customers	Accounting Dept.	5	7	ACT + 7	AC.10.
Audits	Copies of external financial audits with internal workpapers, analyses, and follow-up.	Accounting Dept.	6	7	ACT + 7	AC.10.
Banking	Records of bank accounts and banking activities	Accounting Dept.	3	7	ACT + 7	AC.10.
General Ledger	The general ledger system, including subsidiary ledgers and supporting documentation	Accounting Dept.	10	7	ACT + 10	AC.10.
Payroll	Records of employee hours worked, payments to employees and deductions from them	Payroll Dept.	3	7	ACT + 4	AC.20.
HUMAN RESOURCES						
Benefits Administration	Records of the payment of benefits to employees	Human Resources	EMP	6	EMP + 6	HR.30.
Personnel Files	Official company personnel file including change notices, evaluations, and leave records	Human Resources	EMP	4	EMP + 4	HR.10.
Training	Records of training, testing and certification of employees, including attendance, course materials, and certifications	Safety	EMP	5	EMP + 5	HR.20.

Retention Schedule with Aggregated Legal References

Legal Citations

AC.10. Accounting and Finance					
US	26	CFR	301.6511(d)-1	Limitation of action for claim for refund of general taxes based on bad debt or worthless security is 7 years	7
CA		CL-RTC	19384	Limitation of action for suit against claim for refund denial is 4 years	4
US	26	CFR	1.1081-11	Income taxpayers shall maintain records necessary to substantiate value in property acquired by exchange or barter	Not stated
AC.20. Payroll Accounting					
CA	22	CCR	1085-2 (a) (5) (C) [6]	Employer shall maintain record of cash remuneration paid to each employee in each pay period for 4 years	4
CA	22	CCR	1085-2 (a) (5) (C) [7]	Employer shall maintain record of special payments (bonuses, gifts, vacation pay, etc.) for 4 years	4
CA	22	CCR	1085-2 (a) (5) (C) [9]	Employer shall maintain record of remuneration paid each week to each employee for 4 years	4
CA	22	CCR	1085-2 (a) (5) (C) [4]	Employer shall maintain record of the location where employee services are performed for 4 years	4
HR.10. Personnel Files					
CA	22	CCR	1085-2 (a) (5) (C) [3]	Employers shall maintain records of personnel actions for 4 years	4
US	29	CFR	516.5 (a) [1]	Employers shall maintain personnel files (name, address, birth date, sex, occupation, S.S.#) for 3 years	3
US	29	CFR	801.30	Employers shall maintain polygraph test records for 3 years	3
US	29	CFR	516.2 (a) (1,2,3,4)	Employers shall maintain personnel files (name, address, birth date, sex, occupation, S.S.#)	Not stated
US	29	CFR	516.3 [1]	Employers shall maintain personnel files (name, address, birth date, sex, occupation, S.S.#) of bona fide executive, administrative, and professional employees	Not stated
HR.20. Training					
US	49	CFR	172.704(d)	Employees must maintain records of employee hazmat training for 3 years	5
NV		NAC	618.542(2)(b) [2]	Employees shall maintain training attendance records for 3 years	3
US	29	CFR	1910.66(i)(v)	Employees must maintain records of employee training on powered platforms	3
HR.30. Benefits					
US	29	CFR	4007.10	Administrator of benefit plans shall maintain benefit plan contents for 6 years	6
US	29	CFR	1059	Employers shall maintain employee benefit reports, basic information and data for 6 years	6
US	29	USC	1027	Employers shall maintain all records related to pension plan benefits for 6 years	6

Aggregated Citations Listing

Acme Corporation Records Retention Schedule

Abbreviations: ACT = While Active; EMP = Termination of employment; E = Electronic; M = Microform; P = Paper

	Record Description	Official Custodian	Media	Retention	Legal Reference
ACCOUNTING					
Accounts Payable	Records of amounts owed and paid to outside parties such as vendors and contractors	Accounting Dept.	E	ACT + 7	US 26 CFR 301.6511(d)-1, CA CL-RTC 19384, US 26 CFR 1.1081-11
Accounts Receivable	Records of amounts owed by outside parties such as customers	Accounting Dept.	E, P	ACT + 7	US 26 CFR 301.6511(d)-1, CA CL-RTC 19384, US 26 CFR 1.1081-11
Audits	Copies of external financial audits with internal workpapers, analyses, and follow-up	Accounting Dept.	P	ACT + 7	US 26 CFR 301.6511(d)-1, CA CL-RTC 19384, US 26 CFR 1.1081-11
Banking	Records of bank accounts and banking activities	Accounting Dept.	E,, M, P	ACT + 7	US 26 CFR 301.6511(d)-1, CA CL-RTC 19384, US 26 CFR 1.1081-11
General Ledger	The general ledger system, including subsidiary ledgers and supporting documentation	Accounting Dept.	E	ACT + 7	US 26 CFR 301.6511(d)-1, CA CL-RTC 19384, US 26 CFR 1.1081-11
Payroll	Records of employee hours worked, payments to employees, and deductions from them	Payroll Dept.	E	ACT + 4	CA 22 CCR 1085-2 (a) (5) (C) [6], CA 22 CCR 1085-2 (a) (5) (C) [7], CA 22 CCR 1085-2 (a) (5) (C) [9], CA 22 CCR 1085-2 (a) (5) (C) [4]
HUMAN RESOURCES					
Benefits Administration	Records of the payment of benefits to employees	Human Resources	E	EMP + 6	US 29 CFR 4007.10, US 29 CFR 1059, US 29 USC 1027
Personnel Files	Official company personnel file including change notices, evaluations, and leave records	Human Resources	P	EMP + 4	CA 22 CCR 1085-2 (a) (5) (C) [3], US 29 CFR 516.5 (a) [1], US 29 CFR 801.30, US 29 CFR 516.2 (a) (1,2,3,4), US 29 CFR 516.3 [1]
Training	Records of training, testing, and certification of employees, including attendance, course materials, and certifications	Safety	E	EMP + 5	US 49 CFR 172.704(d), NV NAC 618.542(2)(b) [2], US 29 CFR 1910.66(ii)(v)

Retention Schedule with Direct Citation Linkage

Acme Corporation Records Retention Schedule

Abbreviations: ACT = While Active; EMP = Termination of employment; E = Electronic; M = Microform; P = Paper

	Record Description	Vital Records in this Series (y/n)?	Media	Location or System	Retention	Legal Reference
ACCOUNTING						
Accounts Payable	Records of amounts owed and paid to outside parties such as vendors and contractors	n	E	Software Accounting System	ACT + 7	1, 8, 9
Accounts Receivable	Records of amounts owed by outside parties such as customers	y	E, P	Receivables Dept.	ACT + 7	1, 8, 9
Audits	Copies of external financial audits with internal workpapers, analyses, and follow-up	n	P	Audit	ACT + 7	1, 8, 9
Banking	Records of bank accounts and banking activities	n	E, M, P	Software Accounting System	ACT + 7	1, 8, 9
General Ledger	The general ledger system, including subsidiary ledgers and supporting documentation	y	E	Software Accounting System	ACT + 7	1, 8, 9
Payroll	Records of employee hours worked, payments to employees, and deductions from them	n	E	Software Accounting System	ACT + 4	3, 4, 5, 6
HUMAN RESOURCES						
Benefits Administration	Records of the payment of benefits to employees	n	E	Personnel Office	EMP + 6	10, 12, 17
Personnel Files	Official company personnel file including change notices, evaluations, and leave records	n	P	Personnel Office	EMP + 4	2, 13, , 14, 15, 16
Training	Records of training, testing, and certification of employees, including attendance, course materials, and certification	n	E	Safety	EMP + 5	7, 11, 18

Retention Schedule with Numbered Citation References

Legal Citations

Citation #		Citation	Retention or Limitation Period
1	California	CL-RTC 19384	4
2	California	22 CCR 1085-2 (a) (5) (C) [3]	4
3	California	22 CCR 1085-2 (a) (5) (C) [4]	4
4	California	22 CCR 1085-2 (a) (5) (C) [6]	4
5	California	22 CCR 1085-2 (a) (5) (C) [7]	4
6	California	22 CCR 1085-2 (a) (5) (C) [9]	4
7	Nevada	NAC 618.542(2)(b) [2]	3
8	United States Federal	26 CFR 1.1081-11	0
9	United States Federal	26 CFR 301.6511(d)-1	7
10	United States Federal	29 CFR 1059	6
11	United States Federal	29 CFR 1910.66(i)(v)	0
12	United States Federal	29 CFR 4007.10	6
13	United States Federal	29 CFR 516.2 (a) (1,2,3,4)	0
14	United States Federal	29 CFR 516.3 [1]	0
15	United States Federal	29 CFR 516.5 (a) [1]	3
16	United States Federal	29 CFR 801.30	3
17	United States Federal	29 USC 1027	6
18	United States Federal	49 CFR 172.704(d)	5

Numbered Citation List

Sample Records Inventory Worksheet

Records Inventory Worksheet

Records Series Title	Department
	Division
Also Known As	Location
Is This Records Series Still Being Created? ☐ Yes ☐ No	

Description/Definition of Records Series (Contents, Purpose, Use, Include Form Titles and Numbers, if any)

Type: ☐ Paper ☐ Microform ☐ Bound Volume ☐ Machine Readable (Specify) ☐ Other _____

Size: ☐ Letter ☐ Legal ☐ Other (Specify) _____

Format: ☐ Typewritten ☐ Handwritten ☐ Computer Generated ☐Other _____

Arrangement	Place an "X" in the Proper Column	Yes	No
☐ Alphabetic by _____	Are any COPIES of this records series (or major portion of it) in THIS department?	☐	☐
☐ Numeric by _____	In ANOTHER department?	☐	☐
☐ Chronologic by _____	Does this records series contain classified information requiring SECURITY handling?	☐	☐
☐ Other _____			
Characteristics	Does any legal requirement affect disposal of this records series?	☐	☐
☐ Original ☐ Copy	Does this records series provide data input to an information and records department file?	☐	☐
	Is this records series (or any part of it) ever reproduced on microfilm?	☐	☐
	Stored in information and records department?	☐	☐
Inclusive Dates	Stored on another medium in this department?	☐	☐
From	Does this records series contain Information used in the AUDIT process?	☐	☐
Thru			
	Are these VITAL records?	☐	☐

List All Places Using This Records Series

List All Filing Equipment Associated With This Records Series. (Type of filing cabinet, number of drawers, number of filing cabinets, etc.)

Retention Requirement	Volume in Cubic Feet: _____
Total _____	Rate of Growth: _____
Inventoried By Date	Reviewed By Date

Source: ARMA/Society of American Archivists, *Sample Forms for Archival & Records Management Programs*, ARMA International & Society of American Archivists, 2002.

Sample Records
Survey Worksheet

Survey Worksheet

Respondent Name and Title	Department
	Division
	Location

Section 1. Please list the kinds of records used in your department and provide a brief description for the use of each; and the normal period of business use.

Record	Description	Period of Use
1.		
2.		
3.		
4.		
5.		
6.		
7.		
8.		
9.		
10.		

Source: ARMA/Society of American Archivists, *Sample Forms for Archival & Records Management Programs*, ARMA International & Society of American Archivists, 2002.

Section 2. Are any of the records listed above sometimes needed for other purposes such as audits or lawsuits? If so, list the record, the other use, and the typical time period needed.

Record   Additional Use   Time Period

Section 3. For each of the records listed in section 1, indicate whether the records are paper (P), electronic (E), or mixed media (M).

1.
2.
3.
4.
5.
6.
7.
8.
9.
10.

Section 4. Please list any additional factors you feel we should know about concerning the retention of the records in your department.

Source: ARMA/Society of American Archivists, *Sample Forms for Archival & Records Management Programs*, ARMA International & Society of American Archivists, 2002.

Sample Interview Worksheet

Interview Worksheet

Interviewees and Titles	Department
	Division
	Location

Description/ Definition of Records types in Use (Contents, Purpose, Use, Include Form Titles and Numbers, if any)

Issues Affecting Retention

Operational

Legal

Risk Management

Other

Are these the official copy?　　☐ Yes　　☐ No

If no, where do official copies reside?

How long are these records needed to perform the business function for which they are created and/or used in this department?

What is the consequence of their unavailability?

Source: ARMA/Society of American Archivists, *Sample Forms for Archival & Records Management Programs,* ARMA International & Society of American Archivists, 2002.

Sample Destruction Authorization

Records Destruction Authorization

Records Management

Page # _____

To: (Department)	Location

The records listed below have been microfilmed and are scheduled for destruction upon return of this authorization. Please indicate your acknowledgement below and return to Records Management. Please contact Records Management with any questions regarding this authorization.

Records Description	Date of Records	Retention Authorization

Caution: DO NOT sign this authorization until microfilm is received and has been checked to the department's satisfaction.

Department Approval: I hereby approve the destruction of the above listed records.

Department Chairman	Date

Records Management: I hereby certify that I have this date disposed of the listed records.

Records Management Personnel	Date

Source: ARMA/Society of American Archivists, *Sample Forms for Archival & Records Management Programs*, ARMA International & Society of American Archivists, 2002.

Sample Certification of Destruction

Certificate of Destruction

Company:	
Department:	
Records Coordinator:	Phone:
FAX:	E-mail:
Schedule Issue Date:	

Records Disposed Of:

Records Code	Records Title	Date/Alpha Range

On _____, destruction of the above records was made by means of :

　　☐ Incineration　　　☐ Shredding　　　☐ Other _____

Total # Of Boxes Destroyed: _____

Name _____　　Signature_____　　Date _____

Source: ARMA/Society of American Archivists, *Sample Forms for Archival & Records Management Programs*, ARMA International & Society of American Archivists, 2002.

Standards, Best Practices, and Other Suggested Readings

Standards and Best Practices

ARMA International, *Retention Management for Records and Information*, ARMA International (2005).

International Organization for Standardization, ISO 15489-1 *Information and Documentation—Records Management—Part 1: General*, International Organization for Standardization (2001).

International Organization for Standardization, ISO/TR 15489-2 *Information and Documentation—Records Management—Part 2: Guidelines*, International Organization for Standardization (2001).

Standards Australia, *Australian Standard for Records Management (AS 4390)*, Standards Australia (1996).

Suggested Readings

Books and White Papers

Brown, Gerald F., Robek, Mary F., and Stephens, David O., *Information and Records Management*, 4th ed., Glencoe/McGraw-Hill (1995). (Out of Print)

Isaza, John J., *Legal Holds for "Anticipated Litigation": New Case Developments to Determine Triggering Events & Scope of Production*, ARMA International Educational Foundation, 2007.

Isaza, John J., *Legal Holds & Spoliation*, ARMA International Educational Foundation, 2004.

Montaña, John C., and Cunningham, George C., *Lawyer's Guide to Records Management and Retention*, American Bar Association Law Practice Management Section, 2006.

Saffady, William, *Records and Information Management: Fundamentals of Professional Practice*, ARMA International, 2004.

Skupsky, Donald S., *Records Retention Procedures*, Information Requirements Clearinghouse, 1995.

Articles

Cisco, Susan, "How to Win the Compliance Battle Using 'Big Buckets'," *The Information Management Journal* 42, no. 4 (July/August 2008).

Isaza, John J., "Know When to Hold 'Em, When to Destroy 'Em," *The Information Management Journal* 39, no. 2 (March/April 2005).

Jones, Thomas M., Stevens, David O., and Wallace, Roderick C., "Going Global: Mapping an International Records Retention Strategy," *The Information Management Journal* 42, no. 3 (May/June 2008).

Kahn, Randolph A., "The Risk-Cost Retention Model: Building a New Approach to Records Retention," *The Information Management Journal* 40, no. 3 (May/June 2006).

Man, Elizabeth, "A Functional Approach to Appraisal and Retention Scheduling," *The Records Management Journal* 15, no. 1 (January/February 2005).

Swartz, Nikki, "Putting Retention Management on the Right Track," *The Information Management Journal* 42, no. 6 (November/December 2008).

Torres, Tina, "Creating a Process-Focused Retention Schedule," *The Information Management Journal*, 40, no. 5 (September/October 2006).

Glossary

abandoned property period. A period of time after which things, such as the proceeds of uncashed checks, escheat to the government.

administrative retention criteria. The standards or rules concerned with the availability of records for long-term administrative consistency and continuity, as well as for day-to-day operations of individual program units.

audit. Independent review and examination of records and activities to test for compliance with established policies or standards, often with recommendations for changes in controls or procedures.

audit cycle. The length of time between audits or how often an agency is supposed to perform an audit; every X years.

audit period. A period of time within which an agency can audit an organization's records.

departmental retention schedule. A program-specific retention schedule that is custom-prepared for each program unit in an organization. It lists only those records series that a given program unit maintains with unequivocal retention designations for each.[1]

destruction certificate. A form used to document the destruction of specified records series based on the records retention schedule. Typically includes the records series title, dates covered in the series, organization / agency unit owner of the records series, volume or number of boxes destroyed, name of destruction authorizer, method of destruction, and date of destruction. Also known as a *Certificate of Destruction.*

---

1   William Saffady, *Records and Information Management: Fundamentals of Professional Practice* (Lenexa, KS: ARMA International, 2004), p. 46.

destruction hold. A hold placed on the scheduled destruction of records due to foreseeable or pending litigation, governmental investigation, audit, or special organizational requirements. *See also* **legal hold.**

discovery. The required disclosure of relevant items in the possession of one party to the opposing party during the course of legal action.

destruction. The definitive obliteration of a record beyond any possible reconstruction. *See also* **disposition.**

disposition. A final administrative action taken with regard to records, including destruction, transfer to another entity, or permanent preservation. *See also* **destruction** and **event-based disposition.**

document management (DM). Techniques used to regulate the creation, use, and maintenance of documents according to established policies and procedures.

enterprise content management (ECM). The technologies, tools, and methods used to create, capture, process, store, deliver, and preserve information content, particularly unstructured content, across an enterprise.[2]

event-based disposition. A concept wherein once a registered event occurs, the disposition schedule starts. *See also* **disposition.**

freeze notice. *See* **legal hold.**

frozen records. A suspension of the records destruction process because of special circumstances such as an audit, court order, or investigation. *See also* **destruction hold** and **legal hold.**

functional records schedule. A records schedule that categorizes records by the business function to which they pertain rather than by the program units where they are maintained.

general records schedule. A records schedule governing specified series of records common to several or all agencies or administrative units of a corporate body, which are sometimes characterized as functional retention schedules.

legal hold. A communication issued as a result of current or anticipated litigation, audit, government investigation, or other such matter that suspends the normal disposition or processing of records. Also referred to as **freeze notice, hold, hold notice, litigation hold, preservation order,** or **suspension order.** *See also* **destruction hold** and **frozen records.**

metadata. Structured information that describes, explains, locates, or otherwise makes it easier to retrieve, use, or manage an information resource.

---

2 David O. Stephens, *Records Management: Making the Transition from Paper to Electronic* (Lenexa, KS: ARMA International, 2007), p. 256.

migration. The process of moving data from one information system or storage medium to another. *Note:* Migration is done to ensure continued access to the information as the system or medium is replaced, becomes obsolete, or degrades over time.

office of record. An office designated to maintain the record or official copy of a particular record in an organization.

office retention. The period of time that a records series is to be maintained in active storage for regular use.

permanent record. A record that has been determined to have sufficient historical, administrative, legal, fiscal, or other value to warrant continuing preservation.

physical inventory. The process of identifying all tangible records of an organization. *See also* **records inventory**.

preservation order. *See* **legal hold**.

preservation. The process and operation involved in ensuring the technical and intellectual survival of authentic records through time.

privileged record. A record that contains information that is accessible only to those authorized to view it.

records inventory. A detailed listing that includes the types, locations, dates, volumes, equipment, classification systems, and usage data of an organization's records in order to evaluate, appraise, and organize information. *See also* **physical inventory** and **records survey**.

records series. A group of related records filed / used together as a unit and evaluated as a unit for retention purposes, e.g., a personnel file consisting of an application, reference letters, benefit forms, etc.

records survey. A broad overview of the quantity and type of records within an organization, which is usually completed prior to a detailed inventory. *See also* **records inventory**.

retention period. The length of time a record must be kept to meet administrative, fiscal, legal, or historical requirements.

retention program. A system established and maintained to define retention periods for records in an organization.

retention schedule. A comprehensive list of records series, indicating for each the length of time it is to be retained and its disposition. Also referred to as *records retention schedule* or *records schedule*.

spoliation. The destruction or significant alteration of evidence, or the failure to preserve property for another's use as evidence in pending or reasonably foreseeable litigation, when:

(1) the party having control over the evidence had an obligation to preserve it at the time it was destroyed;

(2) the evidence was destroyed willfully or in bad faith (or in some jurisdictions, negligently); and

(3) the destroyed evidence was relevant to the other party's claim or defense.

statutes of limitation. Laws that set a period within which a lawsuit can be filed over an issue.

total retention. The amount of time a records series is to be stored in active and inactive storage.

trigger event. Something that must occur before a retention period begins to run.

vital records. Records that are fundamental to the functioning of an organization and necessary to continue operations without delay under abnormal conditions.

Index

About The Author

John Montaña is a principal of PelliGroup, Inc., a records and information management consulting firm based in West Point, Virginia. In this capacity, he advises corporations, law firms, and nonprofit organizations on records and information management concerns. His work has included analysis and advice on a wide variety of records and information management issues, including records retention scheduling, the legality of various information storage media, regulatory compliance, litigation and discovery, and other matters likely to impact information management considerations. Montaña also consults with organizations on the analysis, critique, and modification of practices, policies, and procedures, and on retention schedules developed by others, start-to-finish development of records retention schedules, and records management policies and procedures. He is widely recognized as one of the foremost records management experts in the U.S.

Montaña's publications include *Access Rights to Business Data on Personally Owned Computers, Legal Obstacles to E-Mail Message Destruction, Lawyer's Guide to Records Management and Retention, The Sarbanes-Oxley Act: Implications for Records Management*, and *Law, Records and Information Management, the Court Cases*. Additionally, Montaña has written dozens of articles for magazines and professional journals, and he is an active seminar speaker on records management topics. He holds a Juris Doctor from the University of Denver.

About
ARMA International

ARMA International is the leading professional organization for persons in the expanding field of records and information management.

As of February 2010, ARMA has about 11,000 members in the United States, Canada, and more than 30 other countries around the world. Within the United States, Canada, Japan, and Jamaica, ARMA has nearly 120 local chapters that provide networking and leadership opportunities through monthly meetings and special seminars.

The mission of ARMA International is to educate, advocate, and provide resources that enable professionals to manage information as a critical element of organizational operations and governance.

The ARMA International headquarters office is located in Overland Park, Kansas, in the Kansas City metropolitan area. Office hours are 8:30 A.M. to 5:00 P.M., Central Time, Monday through Friday.

ARMA International
11880 College Blvd, Suite 450
Overland Park, Kansas 66210
913.341.3808
Fax: 913.341.3742
headquarters@armaintl.org
www.arma.org